WALTER HOWARD FRERE

by C. S. Phillips

*

THE CHURCH IN FRANCE, 1789–1848
THE CHURCH IN FRANCE, 1848–1907
HYMNODY PAST AND PRESENT

WALTER HOWARD FRERE

Bishop of Truro

A Memoir by

C. S. PHILLIPS

and others

χρώμενος τὸν κόσμον
ὡς μὴ καταχρώμενός

FABER & FABER LIMITED
24 Russell Square
London

*First published in Mcmxlvii
by Faber and Faber Limited
24 Russell Square London W.C.1
Printed in Great Britain by
Latimer Trend & Co Ltd Plymouth
All rights reserved*

ACKNOWLEDGMENTS

This is to make due and grateful acknowledgment to the many who have helped me in the composition of this book. Besides those who have contributed longer or shorter portions of its text, I would particularly thank Mr. John and Miss Audrey Frere for allowing me access to family papers (including a very helpful MS. fragment written by their father, the late Mr. Arthur Frere); Mr. J. L. Stokes, Librarian of Charterhouse School, who has supplied information about Bishop Frere's schooldays there; the Bishop of Chichester (for leave to reproduce part of a letter of Archbishop Davidson), Dr. Claude Jenkins, and various members of the Community of the Resurrection; Mr. A. F. Scholfield, Librarian to the University of Cambridge, for much invaluable help with the List of Writings at the end of the book; the Community of St. Mary the Virgin, Wantage, for permission to reprint prayers; and Mr. A. G. Ferris (of the Ellery Studios, Truro) and Mr. D. Siminson for leave to use photographs. To Fr. E. K. Talbot, C.R., and Dr. H. F. Stewart I owe a special debt for help, criticism and encouragement.

C.S.P.

CONTENTS

CONTENTS

ILLUSTRATIONS

11

1

FAMILY AND TRAINING

by C. S. Phillips

The personality and achievement of the subject of this memoir would provide interesting material for a student of heredity. In him a number of characteristics were blended which seem to be traceable without difficulty to various strands in his ancestry. In appearance and bearing, as also in his profound but gracious reserve, he was very much of an English aristocrat: even when dressed in a shabby old cassock he always looked the most distinguished figure of any company he happened to be in, while his poise and self-command were almost impossible to disturb. It could surprise no one, therefore, to be told that the Freres were an ancient family, presumably of Norman origin, which for several centuries had possessed considerable landed property in East Anglia. Not all aristocrats, to be sure, are 'aristocratic' to look at. But in this particular family lineage and appearance seem to have been well matched. After Walter Frere's death a Stepney incumbent was explaining to two house-painters at work in his vicarage an ancient photographic group in which Frere appeared as a youthful curate. 'Frere?' said one of the men, 'one of the Freres of Roydon? I come from near there myself. Why yes, you can't mistake it. He's got the Frere features—aristocratic, that's the only word for it.'

To this distinction of birth and looks the Freres united remarkable brain-power. For them at least Pope's epigram

13

concerning 'the tenth transmitter of a foolish face' had no sting. Indeed, Walter Frere's father, grandfather and great-grandfather all find a place in the *Dictionary of National Biography*, along with four other Freres of the same generations.[1] It would be interesting to know how this record stands in comparison with other gifted families of commoner rank, especially when Walter Frere's own acknowledged distinction is borne in mind. Two of these Freres had won an exceptionally wide celebrity. One (Walter's great-uncle) was Canning's friend and associate in the *Anti-Jacobin*, John Hookham Frere—described by Coleridge as 'an English gentleman as Spenser dreamed and Sidney realized the ideal'. A diplomat who served as British Ambassador to Portugal and to Junta Spain during the Peninsular War and might later have been Ambassador to Russia, he is much more famous as the translator of Aristophanes. The other was Sir Bartle Frere, the distinguished Victorian proconsul who did

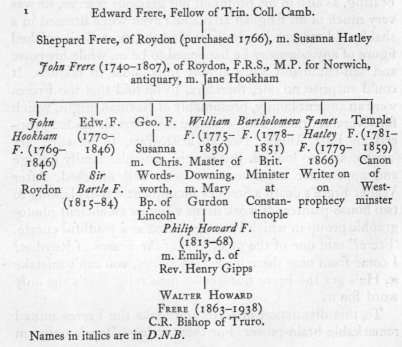

[1] Edward Frere, Fellow of Trin. Coll. Camb.
|
Sheppard Frere, of Roydon (purchased 1766), m. Susanna Hatley
|
John Frere (1740–1807), of Roydon, F.R.S., M.P. for Norwich, antiquary, m. Jane Hookham
|

| *John Hookham F.* (1769–1846) of Roydon | Edw. F. (1770–1846) \| *Sir Bartle F.* (1815–84) | Geo. F. \| Susanna m. Chris. Words-worth, Bp. of Lincoln | *William F.* (1775–1836) Master of Downing, m. Mary Gurdon \| Philip Howard F. (1813–68) m. Emily, d. of Rev. Henry Gipps \| WALTER HOWARD FRERE (1863–1938) C.R. Bishop of Truro. | *Bartholomew F.* (1778–1851) Minister at Constantinople | *James Hatley F.* (1779–1866) Writer on prophecy | Temple F. (1781–1859) Canon of Westminster |

Names in italics are in *D.N.B.*

so much to save British authority and prestige during the Indian Mutiny and, later, to lay the foundations of modern British South Africa—services rather tardily acknowledged after his death by a statue erected by public subscription on the Thames Embankment.

In Frere's immediate forebears this intellectual quality developed the academic bent which stood for one side of his own interest and equipment and made him as well-fitted to be a University professor or College dignitary as for those positions which he actually occupied. His grandfather, William Frere (1775–1836), LL.D. and Serjeant-at-Law, was the first Master of Downing College, Cambridge. As such he was one of the two Heads of Houses then permitted to be laymen, and in his time Downing Lodge was the University's acknowledged social centre. It was from the Master's wife, by the way, that Walter Frere seems to have inherited his musical gifts.[1] Frere's father, Philip Howard Frere (1813–68)—a man of rather unprepossessing exterior, but with great gifts of mind and heart—was Fellow, Tutor and Bursar of Downing and an eminent authority on agriculture (an interest which he can hardly be said to have bequeathed to his younger son). From his great-aunt, widow of the antiquary Sir John Fenn, Philip Frere inherited the main surviving portion of the original MSS. of the Paston Letters.[2] These he sold to the British Museum, and so helped to defray the cost of building the house which he occupied during the last two years of his life, a largish house on the way to Trumpington called for this reason Paston House. A further link with the academic Cambridge of the first half of the nineteenth century was the marriage of the Master's niece, Susanna Hatley Frere, to Christopher Wordsworth (son of an elder Christopher Wordsworth, brother of the poet and Whewell's predecessor as Master of Trinity), who became Bishop of

[1] She had a magnificent voice. Family tradition tells that once, when the great Catalani had a cold, she sang the diva's part for her from the wings. She developed into a remarkable old lady who farmed her own land with great success and smoked a clay pipe.
[2] See D.N.B., s.v. Fenn (Sir John).

15

WALTER HOWARD FRERE

Lincoln in 1869—a saintly and learned divine of whom it was said that 'three quarters of him lived in the fourth century and the rest in heaven'. In this way Walter Frere was linked by ties of cousinhood to the Bishop's two sons— John, the erudite Bishop of Salisbury, and Christopher, Subdean of Salisbury Cathedral, who, like Walter, was a liturgist of note and edited the three fine volumes of the Cambridge University Press edition of the Sarum Breviary.

With the Wordsworths—perhaps the most notable of a select group of families in the nineteenth century born in the ecclesiastical purple—Walter Frere was, of course, connected on the Frere side, not the Wordsworth. But through his mother there flowed into his veins a strain which helped to make him not only a scholar but also an ecclesiastic. Her father, the Rev. Henry Gipps,[1] was appointed canon residentiary of Carlisle Cathedral in 1845, from 1855 onwards holding the living of Crosthwaite as well. Thus the manor house, the courts of Cambridge, and the cathedral close all went to make Walter Frere what he was.

With such antecedents, the future bishop was born on 23rd Nov. 1863. At that time his parents were living at 56 Regent Street, Cambridge; remaining there till Philip Frere's mother, old Mrs. William Frere, died in the following year, when they went to live at her house, Dungate, near Balsham, till Paston House was ready for occupation. Walter was the younger son and second child of a family of four: Arthur, Walter, Ellen (Nelly) and Lucy. At an early age the children lost both parents; Philip Frere dying in 1868 and his wife two years later. This misfortune, while tending to confirm Walter's native independence and self-reliance, may also have induced a certain loneliness of soul that was to be his to the end. 'I sometimes think', he once said to his niece, 'that being an orphan is liable to make you a bit impersonal.'

[1] The Gippses had been a family of standing and substance at Canterbury, or which city George Gipps was M.P. in the second half of the eighteenth century.

By the terms of their father's will the children were put under the guardianship of the Rev. Robert Augustus Gordon, Rector of Barley, Herts, his wife (*née* Elizabeth Lindsay), and another clergyman as co-trustee. It would appear that Philip Frere had once wanted to marry Mrs. Gordon and always retained a high opinion of her intellect and judgment. She was a woman of great beauty, remarkable mental cultivation and imperious will, who was regarded at one time as the heiress to a considerable fortune and had many suitors, including her cousin Alexander, twenty-fifth Earl of Crawford; but in the end she married a penniless curate, while the fortune went elsewhere. She seems to have completely dominated her husband and to have succeeded in commanding a great deal of deference from everybody else.

At the time of their mother's death at Folkestone in 1870, Walter and the two little girls were staying with their Gipps grandparents at Crosthwaite; and Mr. Gordon was unwilling to take them away. The elder boy Arthur, however (he was three years older than Walter), had already gone to school; and it was arranged that he should divide his holidays between Mr. Gordon's rectory at Barley and his Gipps relatives. The three other children had their permanent headquarters under the charge of a governess in a pretty cottage opposite the vicarage gates at Crosthwaite, and thoroughly enjoyed themselves in the lovely surroundings of the Keswick district; but every year they spent part of their summer holidays with the Gordons at Barley.

Among the family papers is a letter written by Walter to Mrs. Gordon on black-edged notepaper at the age of seven— laboriously penned between ruled pencil lines in very large characters. On the second sheet of the paper is an aunt's comment: 'Waltie's penmanship is bad'—a rather surprising start for that handwriting which was to become ever more and more beautiful until it was the very perfection of a scholar's script: something, too, which no amount of writing seemed to affect and which was proof even against the jolting of a train or a motor-car.

B
17

Walter received his first lessons from the governess and also from the aunt just mentioned, Miss Lucy Gipps, a clever and lovable woman who taught him the rudiments of Latin and Greek. In October 1871 she writes to Mrs. Gordon (whom one feels looming over these early years like a remote invalid goddess) that 'Waltie has been a dear little companion to me all these days and I *honestly* think that it is hardly possible to be a better boy'. He was not virtuous to excess, however—indeed a kind of etherealized 'naughtiness' never entirely disappeared from Walter Frere's character. About a year later Aunt Lucy reports: 'Waltie understands very readily—but I must still maintain what I have always said that it requires *great* trouble to get careful work done by him—and he will always *relax* if he possibly can.'

In May 1873 Walter followed his elder brother to the well-known preparatory school situated at Cheam (in Surrey) and usually known by that name; and henceforth he too made his home with the Gordons. His headmaster at Cheam was Mr. Arthur Tabor. A letter from Arthur to Mrs. Gordon describes the first impression he made: 'I am sure you are very glad to learn that Waltie is in the 3d class. He gets on famously among the boys. He is not shy like most new boys are, they generally mumble out their name so that you cannot understand them. . . . Waltie is in the choir and Mr. Hill wants to know if he is going to learn music.' By the end of his first term he was already beginning to distinguish himself. 'Do you know,' Arthur writes home proudly, 'perhaps Waltie will have a speech on speech day, he has learnt it but it is not settled whether he is to say it then or not, but he has learnt it and said it before the whole school. It is quite a wonder. I do not expect a new boy especially one who is one of the smallest in the school has ever said one before. . . . He has also to sing a solo in a solo and chorus.' The performance of the speech duly took place, and Walter's cousin, Lord Monteagle,[1] was present to deliver judgment, noting

---

[1] His father, the Hon. Stephen Spring-Rice, had married Philip Frere's eldest sister, Ellen Mary, in 1839.

incidentally the complete lack of self-consciousness which was always to be one of Walter Frere's most engaging traits. 'I was much pleased with both boys,' he reported afterwards, 'and Waltie's speech (Fluellen and the leek) was given with the most touching naïveté, very different from the more elaborate "art" of the others. . . . Waltie was very much applauded and was perfectly unconscious of anything unusual. I liked [the boys'] looks and ways and was delighted to find I was as good friends as ever with them.' The good start was maintained and Walter steadily made his way up the school. In November 1875 he informs 'Aunt Betty' (Mrs. Gordon), 'Mr. Tabor said he would give a prize to anyone who would say the whole IV book of Horace through which is 542 lines, so I tried and said it and so I am sure of a prize but I have not yet got it'.

From Cheam Arthur Frere was successful in being elected into College at Eton (where both his father and his grandfather had been educated), and in 1876 Walter attempted to repeat the achievement. But he was ill on the day of the examination, and this spoiled his chances. An episode followed that might come from the pages of a Victorian novel. Arthur Frere was accused of being responsible for his brother's illness and failure by giving him wine and making him drunk! To his indignant denials no heed was paid by his guardians; and he was actually removed from Eton as a punishment. Not for many years were his sisters allowed to know the nature of his 'crime'.

As for Walter, he was sent (in Jan. 1877) to Charterhouse, then under the charge of its famous headmaster, Dr. Haig Brown. Here he was elected a Junior Scholar the following July, and a Senior Scholar the next year.

About the end of Walter's first year at Charterhouse a crisis occurred which was to affect considerably the lives and development of the Frere children. Old Canon Gipps died in 1877 (his wife had predeceased him in 1872); and the oversight of the two girls (who were still at Keswick) became a matter of family dispute. The Frere and the Spring-Rice relatives thought the régime of the Gipps aunts too mild, and were anxious to get the girls out of their control. To prevent this Miss Fanny Gipps made an application to the Court of Chancery to have herself appointed in the place of the third of the original trustees, who had died; but Mr. Gordon opposed this, and Lord Monteagle was appointed third trustee instead. Mr. Gordon then decided, with Lord Monteagle's complete approval, to take the girls as well as the boys to live with him at Barley. The result was on the whole disastrous. It always seemed significant that, so far at least as Walter and his sisters were concerned, Mr. and Mrs. Gordon were spoken of in retrospect by their surname, and usually as a kind of collective entity—'the Gordons'. The Bishop (who was one of the least autobiographical people that ever lived) never alluded to those days; but one learned more from his younger sister Lucy (Mrs. Wilfred Barnes), who made it clear that they had left rather a bitter memory in the minds of herself and her sister Nelly. 'For the boys', she once said, 'it was not so bad, as they spent most of their time at school.' Certainly, both Walter and Arthur were the kind of boy that can get much satisfaction out of school life. Yet, even so, some who knew Walter Frere well could not help suspecting that his boyhood had not been a particularly happy one. Here perhaps (given a nature proud, affectionate and sensitive, and inheriting the 'Frere reserve') may be found to some extent the explanation of that intense reticence which not only made it intolerable for him to talk about himself, but also sometimes caused him to go out of his way to head others off from discovering his real grounds of opinion and action—a trait that puzzled not a few and, especially in his last years, diminished the influence that should have been his.

One effect of their experience at home was probably to draw brothers and sisters even more closely together. All their lives they were bound to one another by a deep and constant affection, thus living up to the punning family motto, *Frere ayme Frere*. An illustration of this occurs in a singularly charming letter which Walter sent to Arthur's fiancée on her engagement in 1895. 'Arthur and I,' he wrote, 'as a pair of brothers, have always been a great deal to one another, and though latterly our ways have diverged a good deal and I have become a kind of a dried up old monk, it has made singularly little difference between us.' The same warm affection he extended to Arthur's and Lucy's children. Those in whose brain the 'dried up old monk' idea may have found a lodgment ought to read a letter which he wrote to Arthur's son 'Johnny' when he was two and a half years old, enclosing a lullaby with music specially composed by himself for the little boy's mother to sing to him, and inviting his attention to the 'funny blobs on black lines' in which the music was written. For both 'Johnny' and his sister Audrey he was to be the most delicious and resourceful of playmates —one whose memory has always suggested what a father was lost to the world in Father Frere.

Of Walter's life at Charterhouse there is a good deal more to say than of his Cheam days. A pleasant memory comes back of accompanying the Bishop, in the course of a motor excursion soon after his retirement and some three years before his death, on a visit to Charterhouse during the school's summer holidays, with the special object of examining Sir Giles Scott's imposing new chapel. A flood of reminiscence was not expected, for Frere had nothing of the naïve exuberance of the 'Old Boy'; nor was it forthcoming. But he obviously found a genuine pleasure in revisiting the haunts of his youth. There is no doubt that he was very happy at Charterhouse and enjoyed the best kind of school success, knowing nothing of the misery and frustration of which Mr. E. M. Forster has given so painful a glimpse in his biography of G. Lowes Dickinson of King's, who was an almost exact contemporary at the school. Father Joyce, S.J., remembers him as 'very highly esteemed both by masters and boys— which means a good deal, for boys are sharp critics. He had the reputation of being uniformly courteous and agreeable to all.' Nearly fifty years after he left, in sending a copy of Miss Margaret Thompson's book, *The Carthusian Order in England*, for the school library, he himself was to write, 'It gives me great pleasure to send even so small a gift to a place of which I am so fond and to which I owe so much'.

He was not a school prodigy: both in work and in games his record was good without being brilliant—he did not reach the top flight in either. Intellectually his full powers seem to have been rather slow in maturing, though the wide range of his interests and accomplishments foreshadowed the distinction that was to come. He won a French prize in 1880 and one of the five school-leaving exhibitions (for general subjects) in 1882. In athletics he gained his 2nd XI colours for both cricket and football, was a good fives player, and won the High Jump and second place in the Hurdles in the school sports. His musical gifts were shown to advantage when in 1881 'he conducted' at the school 'a successful Entertainment entirely by indigenous musicians', he himself performing on the piano and 'singing "Toreador" from *Carmen* in the original language'. He rose to be second monitor in his house (Lockites), but was never head. He was also a School Monitor.

Such are the bare bones of Frere's school record. To clothe them with flesh and blood we have a few old photographs portraying a bright and attractive youngster, and the following well-matched vignette from the pen of a Charterhouse friend and contemporary, Sir Laurence Guillemard, G.C.M.G.:

'I have a very clear memory of Walter Frere at Charterhouse. I can, as if it were yesterday, see his eager face, slightly freckled, with the unruly hair perpetually falling over his eyes. I can see his slim active figure, his alert poise, his quick and easy movements. I can hear his high-pitched but gentle voice, his quiet intonation, his merry laughter. He took regular part in all school games and enjoyed them all. It is a pleasure to me to remember that (if I may be excused for blowing my own trumpet) for over two years he and I, as partners in the periodical prize competitions in the fives courts, held a record of unbroken success. Quite recently, on turning out an old cupboard, I found a cup with our two names and the date engraved upon it; and the days of long ago when all the world was young came vividly back to me.

'He was a quite considerable performer in our school sports. I remember especially how one year in the High Jump he cleared the bar at a height which a full-grown athlete would not disdain.

'He had definite dramatic talent, and in our weekly reading parties and occasional more ambitious theatrical performances he always took a leading part.

'So much for his outward and visible characteristics. Of the inward thoughts and beliefs that made their mark later I can say but little. Boys, however well they know each other, rarely discuss their private feelings. They are occupied with day-to-day mundane interests of work and play; they are shy of anything like sentiment, and have no use for the improving discussions indulged in by the young prigs who figure in many stories of school life.

'So Walter kept his thoughts a good deal to himself, however intimate his relations with his friends. But no one who knew him well could fail to realize his earnestness and essential purity of heart. *O si sic omnes!*'

Besides Guillemard, Frere had many other friends at Charterhouse, with some of whom he remained on close terms to the end of his life. Among them may be mentioned Bertram Pollock, Master of Wellington and Bishop of Norwich, and H. K. Southwell, Bishop of Lewes and Provost of Lancing. One of his older contemporaries was the brilliant and eloquent, if rather wayward, Cowley Father, Philip Waggett. It seems a little strange that the two best-known figures for many years in the two leading Anglican religious communities should have both received their nurture at a school so little ecclesiastical in tradition and outlook as the transplanted Charterhouse. Nor was there (as at Harrow in Charles Gore's day) a B. F. Westcott, with his spiritual intensity and much talk of the projected 'Cœnobium', to evoke dreams and ardours in a young soul.

Probably, however, things were just as well as they were —in this particular case, at any rate. Walter was hardly of the impressionable type—he was too critical and fastidious for that: 'All Freres are critical' was a family saying. The spiritual side of his nature (like the intellectual) was to develop very much in its own way and at its own pace. Meanwhile, he had plenty to occupy his time and energies. He did his work and played his games and talked to his friends. His musical taste and ability were encouraged by the headmaster's wife, Mrs. Haig Brown. Very often on Sundays he would go over to the beautiful Surrey village of Wonersh to spend the day with the parson there, who was an old friend of his family. Then, term over, back to his guardian's country rectory on the borders of Hertfordshire and Cambridgeshire, to spend the holidays with his brother and sisters. Here (as perhaps one might expect in the case of a youngster so gifted and with the musician's temperament) he was not always easy company. His sister used to say that it was a great mistake to suppose that his wonderful levelness of temper in later life was a natural endowment: it was much rather a triumph of grace over nature. As a schoolboy and as an undergraduate the beloved 'Wally'[1] was often moody and difficult; refusing to make up a set at tennis when the others wanted one and preferring to retire to his room and bury himself in his books and his music. Music! . . . No one can understand Walter Frere unless he realizes that, next to his religion, his inexhaustible passion for music was perhaps the most fundamental part of him. And in those early years his religious life was in a comparatively embryonic state.

In the autumn of 1882—a month short of his nineteenth birthday—Frere went up to Cambridge, and his real blossom-

---

[1] His name of endearment after he began to grow up. Sometimes also 'Noll'—from a fancied resemblance to a portrait of Oliver Cromwell. One would much like to know *which* portrait!

ing time began. His college was Trinity, where his great-great-great-grandfather had been a Fellow in the early eighteenth century and an adherent of Bentley's, and where also most of his forebears and many of his relatives had been educated. Here he was indeed 'a child of the house'; and certainly no one could have been better fitted to respond to the glories, material and historic, of the magnificent place, or to profit by the opportunities and delights open to an under-graduate, sprung from the ruling class, at one of the older universities in that secure and unclouded world of the Victorian age at its zenith. Nor, for society, was young Frere confined to the wide circle of his college friends. The memory of Downing Lodge and Paston House still lingered in Cambridge; and there were plenty of people in university society to welcome the young man to their houses. Chief of these was Scroope House, the big house just off the Trumpington Road which that tremendous 'character', 'J' (J. W. Clark, Registrar and historian of the University) and his admirable wife made for many years the hub of Cambridge's social life. Here too, at this time and later, Lucy Frere would pay long and frequent visits and give delight by her beautiful singing of Schubert and Brahms. For both brother and sister the Cambridge scene meant a kind of coming 'home'; and all his life Walter loved it and delighted to go back to it. To one who, returning to live there after a lapse of years, found the atmosphere of University society somewhat discouraging, he said, 'Be patient, and you will find that beneath its rather glacial exterior there beats a warm heart.'

Of Frere's time at Cambridge a contemporary and lifelong friend, the Rev. Dr. Hugh F. Stewart of Trinity, Fellow and formerly Dean of Chapel, contributes the following memories:

'I first met him—probably in the rooms of St. John Parry, then Junior Dean—in '84, his third and my second year. The link was certainly music, over which we spent many hours in his fine rooms, Q, Great Court, playing duets and singing. He sang and I accompanied. He taught me to read music, for, an impeccable or at least fearless reader himself, he was without pity for his companion and allowed no pause for the correction of mistakes. The *corpus* of our experiment was mostly Brahms, then at the top of his power; and songs, piano arrangements of orchestral and chamber music were tackled eagerly as they came out. Of course, other classics were not neglected. Walter nearly always called the tune. He was a convinced Wagnerian and tried in vain to infect me with his enthusiasm. Other favourites were Bach, Schubert, Schumann, Mendelssohn for his part-writing and Hubert Parry for the same reason—"the best part-writer since Mendelssohn". (He admired Stanford's skill and learning, but he preferred Parry—held him to be more original.) For Beethoven he had only a moderate enthusiasm; and Chopin he disliked—a weak spot, I think.

'He was in the chorus of the *Eumenides* in 1885, and Stanford, discovering his talent, insisted on making him Secretary of the C.U.M.S. "We must have Frere," he said. I didn't grasp Walter's gifts as a composer until he returned from a week's sick leave (a sharp attack of neuralgia) with a sheaf of songs (Herrick, Shelley, Stevenson, etc.) reproduced by some jellygraph process. Some of these, together with others (Christina Rossetti), were afterwards published, and Stanford thought highly of them.[1] He sang with deep feeling in a strong, rather rough voice and not always perfect intonation, but still most musically. The whole family was deeply musical: Lucy a lovely soprano, Nelly a first-rate pianist, and Arthur a flautist and musical antiquary. Later to Brahms and Wagner Walter added Richard Strauss and Hugo Wolf and the Breton and Greek songs of Bourgault-Ducoudray, which I brought to his notice as to Arthur Frere's, who passed them on to Plunket Greene. These helped to reveal to him the power and beauty of the "modes".

'Between whiles he was learning German, taught by a funny old fellow who used to come two or three times a week

[1] Arthur Frere used to tell how a famous musician (was it Stanford?) once said to him that a composer of distinction was lost when Walter Frere was ordained.

to read Goethe with him. He was soon well equipped for Dresden, where he stayed with the Sonntags, one of whom married G. W. Headlam, brother of the Bishop of Gloucester. He had a real gift for languages, which appeared presently in his mastery of Russian. He spoke French with a very good accent and wrote German idiomatically. His music brought him into touch with Francis Jenkinson[1] (Jinks), with whom he established a firm and lasting friendship. F. J. sat loose to the Faith until he married my sister in 1902. Walter earnestly desired to see him within the fold, and rejoiced when he entered it at last.

'All this was without prejudice to his classical studies, which won him a Major Scholarship and a first class in the Tripos of 1885. In the following year, as a B.A., he began the serious study of divinity, and by way of background he read right through Gibbon. He attended professors' lectures, particularly Dr. Hort's, but mostly read for himself, ranging at will. The marginal notes in his New Testament shew something of his method. Significant of his mood was his organ-practice on the wheezy old instrument in the Round Church, where I would blow for him and listen to his labouring through the prelude to Berlioz's *Faust*.

'We didn't talk religion or theology: we took it all for granted. His own views were old-fashioned High Church, learned from his guardian Mr. Gordon, who was a friend of Mr. Carter of Clewer, who might be seen at his rectory or at the London house the Gordons rented annually. There was nothing in Walter at this period to suggest the heights of doctrine and practice which he afterwards attained. In fact, when I asked him why he was choosing Wells as his theological college rather than (say) Cuddesdon, he said, "I don't want them to make a ritualist of me." At that period he was no ascetic: he enjoyed the good things of life, e.g. luncheon at the Holborn Restaurant between spells of work at the British Museum (this was when he was at Stepney) and a good, small cigar. At college he was a bit of a dandy, sporting

[1] Fellow of Trinity; Cambridge University Librarian, 1889-1923.

a suit of pronounced checks and a red waistcoat of his sister's knitting with great effect. He wore a couple of rings, and agate buttons on his dress waistcoat after the custom of the day. Guided by his brother, a man of the world, he patronized a Bond Street tailor, whom he recommended to his friends. These were especially Hugh Macnaghten, St. Clair Donaldson, Monty Rendall, Arthur Hort, Frank Norris, "Peter" Studd of King's, W. C. Bridgeman, and Stanley Leathes, who, though deaf to music, had a high opinion of Walter's other gifts and recognized that he would have a good claim to a fellowship if such were awarded for general capacity. We stayed together at Cliffe-at-Hoo, Professor Leathes's rectory in Kent, in October '86 and heard there the news of Stanley's own election. But Walter was no philosopher, and I remember the murmur of disapproval which greeted his flippant remark when someone was speaking of Emerson and the Over Soul: "What is the Over Soul?" quoth Walter, "a sort of superior golosh?" As I say, we didn't discuss deep problems and I don't really know what his inner mind was. But he was an assiduous teacher at Jesus Lane Sunday School under the presidency of St. John Parry, to whom, by the by, I owe the surprising statement that at Charterhouse Walter for a time dropped saying his prayers because he didn't see the use of it. We went together to stay with H. B. Chapman (Hugh Macnaghten's cousin) at his parish in Camberwell in '85; and Chapman wanted him as a curate. I remember his being impressed by the spirituality of the Irvingites, whose churches we visited.

'Socially he was a patrician, proud of his family and somewhat arrogant of attitude towards people in his neighbourhood who aspired without right to a county position. But before he left Cambridge he was drawn towards socialism, and this increased when he came to Pusey House and the influence of John Carter.

'He was the most beautiful and the best of friends, whom it is a blessing to have known and a sorrow to have lost.'

To this portrait another Trinity friend, Dr. M. J. Rendall,

28

'WALTIE', *c.* 1876

AT WEIMAR, *c.* 1885

formerly Headmaster of Winchester, adds further details:

'Frere was essentially a modest man, but his gifts and graces soon brought him into contact with the best undergraduates of his time, and also with dons like Jenkinson. . . . I remember well his slim and graceful figure, with athletic and ascetic possibilities: he was quite unlike most of us, as he moved lightly and daintily through life in a cloud of amber and auburn. His attitude to the rest of the world was the reverse of "superior", but some of us felt that we were dealing with a finer and gentler spirit than our own. He played games with enjoyment: he was, indeed, a competent and clever back at soccer, an art which he had learned at Charterhouse; but his game bore no resemblance to the brilliant aggressive tactics of his great contemporary, "Shoot" Walters. Walter Frere was an elusive and gay antagonist whose legs were never at rest: he played nimbly round you rather than at you. It is, I think, characteristic of him that he excelled as a high jumper, which suited his lissom and buoyant figure.

'Intellectually, though a classical scholar of no mean order, he was not in the same rank as Grecian or Latinist with the great Etonians who were at Trinity in his time; but he could hold his own with any in the byways of scholarship classical and medieval: in a "Society" he was a learned and formidable controversialist. . . .

'No one could meet him without feeling that religion was the fundamental principle of his being; but to call him a prig would be absurd. Mirth bubbled out of every corner of him; he enjoyed life, especially cultural life, enormously; but things which were not "of good report" had no meaning for him: they were outside his world.'

At what point in his life Frere definitely decided to take orders we do not know. But what has been said above suggests that it was perhaps during the earlier part of his Cambridge career. In any case, soon after the end of his fourth year at Cambridge he went to Wells Theological College for

a year's theological and devotional training preparatory to
ordination. Dr. Stewart has told us why he went there and
not elsewhere. The reason was characteristic; and indeed
throughout his life (in spite of the vulgar impression of him)
the attitude it expressed held good. It is doubtful if the
advanced Anglo-Catholic section of the Church of England
ever felt quite sure of him. His sister Nelly in later years
would sometimes say, 'Wally, what a Protestant you are
really!'; and the joke was not without an element of truth.
Even his 'ritualism' so called was entirely different from that
of the 'spike': it was historical and devotional, not aesthetic.
Like his friend Gore, he was throughout a staunch 'Church
of England man', for whom the Rome of the Papacy would
for ever cast her spells in vain.[1] Thus, especially at this stage,
the quiet sober Churchmanship of Wells College and its
beautiful and historic setting (so often revisited in later years
through his close friendship with the imposing and erudite
Dean of the cathedral, Dr. Armitage Robinson[2]) must, one
feels, have been exactly what he needed and desired. His
deep regard for the then Principal, E. C. S. Gibson, we
know; for to him, as *Magistro discipulus*, he inscribed his first
large-scale and always best-known book, the rewritten edition
of Procter's *History of the Book of Common Prayer* (familiarly
known as 'Procter and Frere'). Gibson reciprocated the
feeling, once describing Frere to one of his Leeds curates as
'the most brilliant and polished scholar I have ever had the
privilege to train'. As we might expect, besides the routine of
the place he found time for other studies. 'We keep a vast
number of chapels and lectures,' he wrote to Stewart, 'but
also one can do a lot of work on one's own account.' Here
too, above all, we may assume that he laid the foundation of

[1] He told Dr. Stewart about 1900 that it was the Pope that made it
impossible to go over to Rome.
[2] In his *Recollections of Malines* Frere tells how, when the three Anglican
representatives alighted at Malines railway station on a dark December
evening before the First Conversation, the Dean's tall striking figure and
large hat caused him to be mistaken for Cardinal Mercier by some bystanders
who fell on their knees to receive his blessing.

that strong spiritual life and unsparing self-discipline which, while retaining all that was fine and attractive in the brilliant young Charterhouse and Trinity man, was to make him so shining an example of 'a dedicated spirit'. Of the way in which he won through we know nothing; for he has not told us, nor is it even imaginable that he should. But *post hoc propter hoc* is not always an unsound guide; and we are fairly safe in surmising that in the secret memories of the full-grown Walter Frere Wells held a very special place.

2

STEPNEY AND RADLEY

by C. S. Phillips

Walter Frere was ordained deacon in St. Paul's Cathedral at the Advent ordination of 1887 by Bishop Temple of London. His ordination as priest followed in 1889.

His first and only curacy was at the parish church of Stepney (St. Dunstan's) under the then Rector, Edwyn Hoskyns, who later became Bishop of Southwell, and towards the end of his life succeeded to the family baronetcy. With him and his kindly if at times rather formidable wife Walter's relations were of the happiest, and in later years he was always delighted to have a chance of seeing them again. Hoskyns had a great reputation as a parish priest, and gathered round him a remarkable succession of curates. In Frere's time the staff comprised, besides himself, his cousin Frank Gurdon, later Bishop of Hull, and a Wells contemporary named Hudleston. With the latter he set up housekeeping in what he described proudly in a letter as 'my own hired house, that messuage, tenement, etc. (*vide* my lease just signed) known as 24 High Street, Stepney'. Near by at Bethnal Green was one of his closest friends at Trinity, St. Clair Donaldson, later Archbishop of Brisbane and Bishop of Salisbury.

Those eighties of the last century were great days for the Church of England—a time when perhaps its personnel was more variously distinguished and its influence on the national life more truly effective than at any other. And, not least,

great days in the East End of London. Toynbee Hall,
Oxford House and various College missions were gathering
their first fruits; and the leading churches of East London
were staffed, like Stepney, by able and hard-working men
who made them centres of a vigorous and well-organized
religious life. The optimistic young Head of Oxford House,
Arthur Winnington-Ingram, could even venture not many
years later to sound in the ears of Cambridge undergraduates
the cry of Caleb to the Israelites on the borders of the
Promised Land: 'Let us go up at once and possess it, for we
are well able to overcome it.'

In such an atmosphere and with such associates a keen
young deacon, with the dew of the theological college still
fresh on him, might be expected to develop a strong pastoral
zeal and understanding and love of souls—qualities which in
Frere's case, for all his learning and other interests, were to
continue unabated to the end. 'An East London Correspondent,' writing in the *Church Times* after his death, recalled
how 'on the Sunday evening that the newly-ordained slim
ascetic deacon read himself in, Walter Frere started on his
great spiritual career.' Rather more than a year later Frere
himself could write to Hugh Stewart: 'The work and interest
of the place grows on one very much here: the more one does
the more there is to do, and the more one enjoys it: and now
we are such a lively trio here that it is impossible to get into
the dumps which seem to be the curse of East End labours.'
Archdeacon F. N. Thicknesse (in those days Rector of Lime-
house) writes: 'Frere and Gurdon came to Stepney about the
same time, and both of them made a distinct impression in
the neighbourhood—Frere made the greater impression of
the two.' He also records an amusing story of a Stepney
parishioner saying: 'The Rector o' course 'e's all right; but
that there long 'un 'e ain't no better than a Cartholic, and the
short thick 'un 'e ain't much better.'

At Stepney Frere's work lay in that part of the parish
which is now the parish of St. Faith. A former vicar of this,
the Rev. Noel Brown (an old Mirfield man), has told how

'Frere took the district to heart, and it remained in his heart to the end. Forty years later he not only remembered the names of the streets but the names of countless people. ... St. Faith's was the dream of Hoskyns; but it was mainly due to Frere that the dream came true. There was a little school room in Shandy Street, but Frere was most at home on the rubbish heap on which in 1891 the church was built. There, amid the old scrap iron, the rusty kettles and the tin cans he began that ministry of the word which by its depth and simplicity was to be such a power in *Ecclesia Anglicana* for the next few decades.'

The 'East London Correspondent' already quoted records that it was Frere who at St. Faith's 'suggested the then unknown hour of 9.30 for the parish Communion, thus, as he said, giving a chance to the family of worshipping together, and then going home to prepare the Sunday dinner'. To which, perhaps, Dr. Stewart may append a footnote:

'Obedient as he was, at Cambridge and certainly later, to all good customs of the Church, I don't believe he ever regarded the *strict* fast before Communion as an *essential*.[1] He valued early celebration because it avoided the heavy Sunday breakfast and intrusion of worldly business in what should be preparation for the Eucharist. 9 a.m., he said to me, was an ideal hour for it, calculated to unite without distracting. He was, if I may say so without offence, the most reasonable of all the Anglo-Catholics of my acquaintance.'

Frere's activity at Stepney was not exclusively of the ecclesiastical kind. Dr. Stewart has told us already of the socialist bent which he began to follow at the end of his Cambridge time, and has kept a letter in which, soon after leaving Stepney, Frere wrote, 'I am preaching rank Socialism to *the* fasl able congregation of Oxford in compressed doses of twenty minutes.' This 'bent' he retained to the end of his life. His 'socialism', however (perhaps better spelt with a

---

[1] A distinction, one imagines, should be drawn here between his own practice and what he might be ready to allow to others. See also the letter printed on pp. 137 ff.

small than with a large s), was a very different thing from the modish Socialism of to-day. It was the 'Christian Socialism' of the early nineties—idealistic and religious to the core, ethical far more than political, rooted in 'compassion for misfortune, as such': less the comfortable vision of a 'planned society' than a call to personal self-sacrifice. It was, in short, precisely the state of mind which (as we shall see) helped to turn Walter Frere into a 'monk'. Thus when in his Truro days angry Cornish squires thundered from time to time, 'The Bishop is nothing but a d——d Socialist!', they failed to realize how slightly absurd their accusation sounded in the ears of those who knew the offender well, or that, when others were involved, the Bishop simply intervened to maintain the right of one of his clergy to express, not his Bishop's views, but his own. But, unlike most savants, he was keenly concerned with what went on in the great world outside and anxious to find a remedy for its cruelties and injustices. Thus (to quote 'East London Correspondent' again) 'Frere was elected to the local Board of Guardians, where his zeal was at times overpowered by the traditional outlook of Bumbledom.'

Besides his pastoral and social work, Frere also found time for study. Dr. Stewart writes:

'Here he began historical research (*Memories of Stepney Parish*, 1891)—his first excursion into history was with his brother in a history of Barley parish. His hours of leisure were spent at the British Museum, and he was very soon involved in the labyrinth of Plainsong, of which by 1894 he was a master. He took his cue in liturgical study from Henry Bradshaw, whom he didn't know at close hand, but whose methods he adopted. We went together to H.B.'s funeral in Feb. '86, and he gave me the mezzotint from Herkomer's portrait.'

Along with his intellectual went his spiritual development. Here (as at Wells) we have no knowledge of the process, but only of the result—especially his crucial decision (before the end of 1891) to throw in his lot with the newly founded and still highly experimental Community of the Resurrection. A precious relic, however, of his power to link together his learning and his devotion survives in a shabby leather-bound copy of P. G. Medd's edition of Bishop Andrewes' Greek *Devotions*[1] in the original language, inscribed on the title-page 'Walter Howard Frere, 1892', i.e. soon after he left Stepney to join the Community. On the blank pages bound in he has written, in exquisite shapely scripts without blot or erasure, a considerable amount of material of his own, a good deal of it consisting of centos after the manner of Andrewes himself, and all of it in Greek, Hebrew or Latin. (It may be noted that, like his father, he said his daily psalms in Hebrew.) This material was evidently inserted over a long period of years, and it seems not impossible to distinguish various 'strata'. So intimate a record is hardly for the general eye; but perhaps a biographer may lift the veil for a moment from what seems, judging by the handwriting, to belong to the earliest stratum of all—a kind of bede-roll in Latin headed *Commemoratio Temporalium*, with names indicated by initials. The list of those to be prayed for begins with his parents, brothers (one dead in infancy) and sisters, and goes on to enumerate *Tutores* and *Nutritores*. It continues thus (his friends at least will guess many of the names):

Magistri	EL. CCT. WHB.
Benefactores	TS.†
scriptis	LA.† JT.† EBP.† AJM.

[1] In these Stepney days Frere gave Hugh Stewart a well-worn copy of the 1848 Pickering edition of the *Devotions*, bound in 'ecclesiastical calf' the worse for wear, and inscribed as follows:

Hugoni Fraser Stewart
hoc volumen
visui sane satis deforme
intellectui autem animaeque Xtianae valde pulchrum
et fructuosum opus antistitis n̄ri
d.d.
W. H. F.
sibi indigno preces obsecrans
suas invicem quantulascunque daturus
MDCCCLXXXIX
in Festo Exaltationis S̄ctae Crucis

concionibus	HBC.
exemplis	ECSG. EH. FG.
amicitia	HFS. StCD. RStJP.
colloquiis	BP. VSSC. MCB. PB.
monitis	LSW. CG.

and ends with *reprehensione* and *injuriis* (no initials to this last).

2

Once in the course of a conversation the Bishop was speaking of the two kinds of ability necessary for the successful launching of a religious community or indeed of any other corporate venture—those of the 'pioneer' and the 'consolidator' respectively; adding that it was seldom that both were united in the same person. We were discussing an altogether different case; but perhaps the thought of his own Community was not wholly absent from his mind. Charles Gore, then in his thirties and wielding an almost prophetic sway in Oxford as one of the three Librarians of the Pusey House, was not only the founder of the Community of the Resurrection and the guide of its infant footsteps, but also (it is hardly too much to say) the prime creator of its specific ethos. Yet after not many years, on becoming Bishop of Worcester (1901), he ceased to be a member of it; and the work of 'consolidation' was left to other hands.

It is unnecessary to do more here than to summarize briefly the story of the Community's beginnings, which is told more fully in Dr. Prestige's *Life of Bishop Gore*.[1] It was a development (contemplated from the first) of a devotional association of clergymen formed in 1887 under the name of the Society of the Resurrection, having its founder Gore as its elected Superior and its centre at Pusey House. Here in 1889 seven of the members took up residence and engaged in an examination and discussion of monastic rules Eastern and Western, past and present. A provisional rule was formu-

[1] See Vol. I, pp. 106 f., 137 f.

lated, and four persons signed acceptance of it for one year
—Gore himself, William Carter, James Nash and John Carter. This situation continued till 1891, when William Carter
left to become Bishop of Zululand and two new recruits
arrived—Cyril Bickersteth and George Longridge. At the
end of the same year Frere had got far enough to be able to
write to Hugh Stewart: 'I go to Oxford (leaving here for
good on [Jan.] 14th) about the end of the month to see what
they are up to with their brotherhood'—a characteristic way
of intimating what another might have described as his
'resolve to test his vocation to the religious life'. The total
number was thus brought up for the present to six—the
primal nucleus of the Community. All six were professed
together in the chapel of the Pusey House on St. James's
Day, 25th July 1892.

Frere's reasons for joining we are left in the main to conjecture for ourselves; but he told his friend Stewart at the
time that he wanted to supply a Cambridge element in the
undertaking, and that he felt that the country clergy needed
help and that the parochial system was insufficient. Many
years later he gave a further reason to another friend, Fr.
Bernard Horner: 'The thing that as much as anything
brought me to the Community was the feeling that it was
intolerable for me to possess money.' (There seems good
reason to believe that practically the whole of his patrimony
was absorbed by it.) In any case, from the outset it must have
been clear to the others, if not to himself, that he was likely
to be an important factor in the venture. He was, indeed, the
only one of the original band who was undazzled enough,
and strong enough, to stand up to the founder. And stand up
he did when he felt that the occasion required it—though,
certainly, no pair of men ever had a vaster respect for one
another than those two.

For the moment, however, all were agreed as to the desira-
bility of trying out the new experiment in an atmosphere less
hectic and distracting than that of Oxford. The opportunity
came when Gore was offered in 1893 the living of Radley, a

small and beautiful Thames-side village five miles south of Oxford on the way to Abingdon. The benefice, which had a microscopic income, had always been a 'donative' dependent on the lord of the manor; and it was characteristic of Gore that he refused to accept it until its position was regularized by a formal marriage to the diocese. There was a charming little church, full of beautiful old things; and almost touching it was the vicarage—once described by Gore, when Bishop of Oxford, to the present writer (who had recently become vicar) as 'two houses connected by a very imperfect join'. The original building was a picturesque, half-timbered structure of early Tudor date looking out on a shady lawn. To this, at right angles, had been added in the 1870's a tall and typically Victorian box of bricks, facing due north and full of varnished pitch-pine within. In this habitation, which over twenty years later was still innocent of any kind of modern convenience, the infant Community settled down to find out what it was made of.

Against such a background, then, we are to imagine the kind of existence of which Canon Campbell Crum contributes the following sketch:

'It is fifty years, all but two, since I saw the Bishop in the days of the Community of the Resurrection at Radley. They lived in the vicarage and, for sleeping, some overflowed to a neighbouring farmhouse. There was Charles Gore, who seemed to me the St. Anselm of our modern days. And there were "Walter", and "George", and "Cyril", and "John", and "James", and "Richard", and "Paul", and "Gerard". The rest were all younger men than Gore, who had consented to be called "the Senior". I remember being told how he had "writhed" himself free of any title which claimed anything but age in which he had advanced beyond the others. It would be quite unendurable to be called "the Superior".

'They were all of them, I suppose, dissatisfied with the opportunities which a conventional round of parochial duty affords for the kind of life which, in the Middle Ages, would have been called a "religious" life. The venture was fairly new then at Radley. Gore had begun as vicar there, and, I imagine, had been rather restless as a vicar. Then he became canon of Westminster; and the duties of the village vicarage were taken over by James Nash, afterwards Coadjutor Bishop of Capetown. He was always in residence; and the two who were oftenest at the vicarage with him were Gerard Sampson and Paul Bull. Only at intervals they would all be there: all the nine.

'I wonder how anything can be so inexhaustibly interesting and wonderfully diverse as those characters—the lights and reflexions which two of us, laymen, were privileged to live among. For from time to time two young men, on the way from the University towards ordination, were admitted to be living and reading there: two "Y.G.s". "Y.G." was short for "young gentlemen"; for the housekeeper and her husband called us that. It was Gerard who convoked the Community, ringing the church bell: tender-hearted, contemplative, the mystic of the company, I'll say. Less emaciated than Gerard, less solemn in conversation was Paul. He and Walter had been out together, two and two. Paul, less gently patient than James, who was in charge of the parish. They were James's flock; and it was not easy for Paul to preach to them. And Gerard preached fairly often too. Did he like to preach? was he nervous? He told me: "Mind, preaching is a great pleasure. It is like drinking good champagne."

'And "Walter" preached there, and at neighbouring churches. I don't think he was conscious of the tension which was a mutual discipline to Paul and James. He would seem to be speaking quite naturally to people, saying quite simply what he thought and saying it as if his hearers had as good a right as he had to hold their own honest convictions. He had the kind of candour which comes from a conviction that all will work out well if an honest man speaks honestly to honest men. He was no partisan. You felt the truthfulness of him. He came in one day when I was reading a Church of England history which gave, as it seemed to him, a faulty account of the Donation of Constantine. The name of the historian, if I chose to remember it, is a venerable name; but the glamour faded from his fine prose. When Frere spoke, I felt ashamed, and almost afraid, for him.

'My fellow Y.G.—if I were talking to him and not writing to you—would remember with me, with some gaiety, occasions on which we were provoked to a mirth which must not betray itself, by oddities of speech and dress and manner of men who were too deeply in earnest to be thinking how they appeared to us; but, if we talked of Walter Frere, there would not be the slightest suspicion of mockery within a mile of our memory. I think one looked at Frere as you look at some statue or picture which others tell you is beautiful, and you are finding out that they are right to say so. We never even smiled at Walter: only with him, never at him. We may have enjoyed his wit, but we took himself always with serious respect. It may have been that his ideas were, so many ways, foreign to me. Maybe we saw him as a man who was doing something which could never be ludicrous. There was his immense scholarly knowledge of the past: "tropers" and "graduals" were only indications of an order of life which it is a great loss, however unconscious a world may be of it, to be unable to recapture.

'Radley was an experiment. Here was a Community, each working in his own way, each in some sense a specialist and coming home for peace and renewal to that brotherhood, with their regular life: very unworldly people. Silence was observed until noon. They made their own beds. Some, sometimes, smoked. Some never did. Sometimes the Senior would read a book, or read aloud. Some of the talking was, I should say, very "good" talking: not competitive but, if I were the umpire, I should award the prize to the talking of the Senior and Walter Frere.

'Sometimes we were few at home: say, James and Gerard and the Y.G.s. And James, I dare say, would find Walter at the piano and playing to us and singing. I don't know how well he did it. I know we four were a very unmusical lot.

41

But about that too I felt he had a certain distinction. I have suggested that he seemed to me in some ways like a beautiful white marble Apollo statue. This would be an hour of the unbending of the bow. Not very far off was the feeling of respect for the bow: a bow which could, one felt, shoot far and aim true.

'If "Isaak" Y.G. and I had our doubts about him, they were doubts about his wisdom as a bodily man in this sub-lunar world. How much sleep did he allow himself? His face —it was a beautiful face—shewed signs: in the eyelids there was the suggestion of overworked eyesight. I thought of Thomas Erskine of Linlathen saying to John Macleod Campbell, "Be kind to the body, Campbell. Be kind to the body." But that was in another generation far from Oxford, and the Oxford Movement.'

After this fashion, then, the fledgling Community tried and strengthened its wings till it should be ready for bolder flights. At last, after four years, it quitted in January 1898 the idyllic environment of the quiet Berkshire vicarage to settle in one that was the opposite in all respects—a big, solid and exceedingly ugly house of smoke-grimed stone at Mirfield in the heart of industrial Yorkshire, built by a rich mid-Victorian manufacturer and called Hall Croft, which was to be the nucleus of its permanent home. Here too, before long, Frere was to begin the great creative period of his life, to which Truro was no more than an epilogue. But that story must come from another hand.

MIRFIELD

by Father E. K. Talbot, C.R.

Walter Frere differed from the other original members of the Community of the Resurrection. For one thing, he alone was a Cambridge man, and not Oxford itself could have given him an Oxford mind. Nor is there any reason to think that he had, with the others, fallen under the potent personal influence of Charles Gore, or that the founder of the Community had inspired his religious and theological outlook. The two men had by nature little in common. They shared indeed a steadfast adherence to the Catholic Faith, an unshaken loyalty to the English Church, a devotion to learning, a sensitiveness to social injustice, and a zealous solicitude for individual souls. In some other respects they were at one: for instance in an impatience with the *mesquineries* of the ecclesiastical mind, and in a zest for the exploration of historic sites and buildings. But in temperament, intellectual interests, and manner of discourse they were notably diverse. The emotional sensibility that gave to Gore's moral and prophetic fervour so great an intensity was absent from Frere's cool and dispassionate disposition. The troubled sadness that looked out of Gore's eyes made no appearance in Frere's. A deep 'proximate pessimism' (to use a phrase of von Hügel's) coloured Gore's vision of the world, and was audible as an undertone even in his humour. Frere's glance betrayed no such sombre brooding. Accepting the world as he found it, in all its confusions, cross-purposes and incongruities, he cheerfully addressed himself to each successive step ahead through the maze of circumstance. Gore and Frere differed greatly also in bent of mind. The former's interest ranged over a very wide field of literature, both of prose and poetry. Frere read little outside the sphere of his own special studies. Metaphysical speculation and religious philosophy won from Frere the slightest possible attention: and, unlike Gore's, his mind was but little engaged in the problems of theology. Even in the method of their converse they stood in strong contrast. Lightly Frere would touch a subject with swift and pointed comment and with an economy of words, where Gore would engage it with the slow and intricate elaboration of a rich vocabulary.

It was not therefore as one more disciple to a great teacher that Walter Frere was drawn to the Community. There was a touch of caution in the words that marked his first approach to it. 'I am going to see what these Oxford men are up to.' He came as one to whom the call to the Religious Life was paramount and who was bent upon pouring his life into its mould. Probably there were particular considerations that reinforced this central determination. Historical appreciation of the part played by the Religious Orders through the ages in raising and re-animating the life of the Church; a spontaneous attraction of his spirit to the liturgical patterns of the Divine Office; a strong impulse to disencumber himself of personal possessions and to find contentment in simplicity; a resolve to fill his time with dedicated industry and to find in obedience the mortification of a will inclined to be imperious: all these may well have contributed to his submission to the Religious yoke. But they were only elements comprised in a single purpose—to find freedom in the service of God under a Religious Rule. The presence among the first professed in the Community of one over whom the personal sway of the founder had less emphatic power than over the others was of great significance for its future development. The foundations were laid and they abide: the main principles of the Rule were established from the beginning and by them the distinctive ethos of the Community has been determined, and it persists through the changes of times and persons. But it would have been difficult for the Community to discover and pursue its proper development had it remained within the orbit of one whose endowments already at the time of the Community's foundation marked him inevitably for a public life in Church and nation. It was to be Frere, for whom all other purposes and interests were subordinate to those of the Religious Life, who was to lead the Community in the most formative stages of its growth and expansion. The first years had already revealed the opportunities and needs in the Church's life which the new Community might meet, and there was a youthful zest in its members to meet them. But they revealed also the perils that threatened its nascent existence. Its common life could easily be dissipated by multitudinous claims made from outside upon the energies of individual brethren: and a life so weakened at the centre could hardly attract and hold new recruits to the Religious Life. There was a danger of it remaining a group of friends borne along in the wake of Gore's own course—strongly as he disclaimed any absolute control of the lives of the others. His passion for genuineness, his fear lest appearance should out-pace inward reality, impelled him to protect the Community by a wholesome unobtrusiveness. It was not to pretend to be more than it was, nor claim to be more monastic than the facts warranted. It was to foster indeed with zeal its inner life; but in outward guise and in terminology it was to be restrained and modest. But this very reserve obscured to the world outside its Religious character and intent. And the Community itself was likely to suffer from an insufficiently distinctive embodiment of its spirit and ideals.

In these circumstances Walter Frere's misgivings were soon audible. His conception of the Community reached out beyond the Oratorian idea envisaged by Gore. He saw clearly that its Rule already required a more closely-knit common life, and that this was endangered by the scattered activities of the small number of brethren. 'We are in peril of finding

45

ourselves not monks but hermits.' He strongly opposed the
establishment of a House in Little Cloisters when in 1894
Gore accepted a canonry of Westminster. The Community
was not strong enough to bear such a dispersal of its members. Moreover, neither Radley nor Westminster provided
the right setting for its development. The one was too
Arcadian, the other too full of 'prelatical splendour'. 'Poverty
and obscurity are what we want, and really Westminster is
enough to stifle anyone's religion.' (Be it remembered that
this was the Abbey of fifty years ago.) 'Both Radley and
Westminster are too respectable to attract the sort of person
we want, and if we don't take care we shall become a little
body of middle-aged clergymen of unimpeachable respecta-
bility, polite manners, and various sorts and degrees of individual usefulness: but no community—much: no poverty—
much: no obedience—much: everything in fact that Archdeacon Farrar would like to see. *Absit omen.*' Both the monk
and the aristocrat in Frere protested against such a prospect.

Concentration of spiritual energies, the practice of the
common life, growth in stability, appropriation of the principles of the Religious Life, and an outward order accordant
with those principles—these were the necessities that Frere
saw to be requisite if the Community was to take root down-
ward and bear fruit upward. With these ends in view he welcomed Gore's own long-nourished desire that the Community should live and work in the industrial North: and the
move to Mirfield in 1898 opened the way to the Community's real consolidation. The house—surprised to find its
mundane ugliness appropriated to a monastic establishment
—was well sited and suited for the Community's purposes.
Surrounded by ample and beautiful grounds, it was sufficiently withdrawn to ensure quiet, and yet had excellent
communications to facilitate the work undertaken by the
brethren. Finally purchased in 1902, it became the Mother
House of the Community. The first Superior was, to be sure,
still at Westminster during these years, perhaps the most
fruitful of his prophetic ministry. But this somewhat incon-

THE YOUNG COMMUNITY, MIRFIELD, 1901

Left to right: Top row, John Carter, Walter Frere, Clement Thomson; 2nd row, Waldegrave Hart, Charles Gore ("Senior"), Charles Fitzgerald; 3rd row, George Longridge, Richard Rackham, Gerard Sampson, Cyril Bickersteth; bottom row, Samuel Healey, James Nash

'THE FOUR SUPERIORS'

Left to right: Bishop Frere, E. K. Talbot, Bishop Gore, G. Longridge

gruous arrangement was to end when Gore accepted the Bishopric of Worcester. It is significant that Frere, holding that the claim of the Religious Life had a priority over all others for those who embraced it, opposed the idea of Gore becoming a bishop and severing his membership in the Community. When in turn, much later, he himself was pressed to accept the Bishopric of Truro he only consented on condition that he was allowed to remain a full member of the Community and that it could establish one of its houses at Truro. However, in the first case the decision was left to Gore himself, who found himself unable in conscience to refuse the bishopric: and he was released from his Community obligations. Subsequently provision was made to enable him to maintain his Religious vocation by his election as Prelate-Brother in the Community.

Thus ended the period of the Community's infancy under the dominating influence of the man who under God had brought it to birth and whose commanding voice is still audible in its Rule. It would not be untrue to say that the interior development of the Community has been determined by the endorsements or qualifications which experience has wrought upon the principles represented by its founder. The way was now open for the hand of a master-builder to do his constructive work upon the foundations securely laid. Walter Frere was elected Superior in January 1902: and save for a period of three years, 1913–1916, when Father Longridge was Superior, he was to hold office until 1922.

The qualities which Walter Frere brought to his task were of inestimable value to the Community. In purpose and habit of life he was, first and last, a Religious. The constraint of his vocation informed his whole being and welded it into unity and stability. 'The first thing and the last thing required of every Religious is stability—or "steadfastness", to use the Bible term. All specific obligations and vows have this for their end.' So he wrote: and himself exemplified the truth. But the stability was matched by a singular flexibility—like that of a finely-tempered blade. There was nothing rigid about him. Stability and freedom reinforced one another in him. Just because his heart was fixed in a continuing inward intent he could move with a liberty that had something in it of an ordered dance. It seemed sometimes that he under-rated the need that others less detached and free have of external bonds to preserve their stability. Thus he could rest more content than others with the absence from the earlier form of profession in the Community of specific vows because his own intention of steadfastness was so unreserved. But there was no mistaking the impress of religious dedication upon the multifarious energies of his life. And this was the more notable because it controlled a mind naturally tempted, it may be surmised, to be impatient, wilful, fastidious, even a touch scornful. The secret of his liberty and gaiety was a steely discipline. Ascetic he was, in the true sense of that word—one trained and stripped to move freely at the behest of the Will that controlled him. No one could look at him without perceiving that he knew the meaning of bodily aus-terity. But of this he would sometimes speak lightly. Speak-ing of the principle of mortification he would say that many think that that has all to be worked out in the body. 'That will carry you a little way but not very far: alone it may land you in subtle perils. But what has ceaselessly to be mortified is self-will.'

To this central point of detachment he addressed himself unremittingly. So blithe, so easy and light was the way of him that you might miss this secret of his spiritual greatness. In a pre-eminent degree, one may dare to say, he was dead to self. No vanity tarnished his attainments: under disappoint-ment no note of self-pity quivered in his voice: self-concern never seemed to taint his motive or divert his aim. One example of this detachment from self may be given. On his return home one day from a long absence one of the brethren offered to carry his bag up to his room, and asked him whether there was not another. 'There was,' he replied, 'but it has disappeared. Someone took it the other day from the platform where I had put it down for five minutes, and it cannot be traced.' Asked what it had contained. 'Oh! some papers,' he replied lightly: and it was only further enquiry that disclosed the fact that 'some papers' were the finished manuscript of a book on which he had been engaged for twenty years. For three or four weeks the bag seemed to be irretrievably lost, until it was returned from America by someone who, quite innocently, had snatched it up by mistake for his own and embarked with it at Liverpool. Yet during those days, as far as one could see, Frere betrayed no sign of irritation nor allowed any shadow to pass upon his habitual brightness. It was as if he were saying, 'Well, that's that—what is the next thing God wants me to do?' And that was typical of much else in his life.

This detachment was manifest in his astonishing industry, in the swiftness with which he could lift his mind from one absorbing occupation to another, in his unruffled patience in face of provocation, and in the generosity with which he put his superior knowledge at the disposal of others. To a mind as nimble and quick as his the slow fumbling of others must often have been a weariness and a bore. Yet he rarely betrayed any sign of ennui.

The cost of such inner discipline was apparent when in the last years of his life physical weakness and weariness loosened a little his powers of self-command. One got glimpses of the natural impatience which habitually he had controlled with such grace, and of which memory fails to recall any exhibition during the long years of his Superiorship.

The stamp of the true Religious was further revealed in the genuineness with which Frere embraced the counsel of poverty and simplicity of life. Endowed as he was by nature with all the capacity for a life of refined and humanistic culture, he not only endured but loved spareness, and was unhappy with superfluity. He rarely sat in an easy chair: and those who travelled with him on holiday will know how relentlessly he sought out the humblest inns to stay in—not always to the satisfaction of his companions. Characteristic of him were the warnings he uttered to the Community against not only an individual but a corporate possessiveness, a danger which in history has beset flourishing religious communities. Even the installation of electric light in the Mother House drew from him a fear lest the Community should insensibly slip into luxury. And proposals to secure its financial security aroused his most caustic comments. In his Commentary on the Rule he writes: 'First God endows us with an instinctive appreciation of the good of this world: then he induces us by a sanctified self-interest to surrender the good things of this world for the better things of the heavenly state: but beyond this our Blessed Lord teaches us by His own example to love surrender for its own sake, and for His sake as chiefest and best of all.' That reflects his own spirit. Certainly there was nothing grim or strained in his austerity. Rather, it gave an unencumbered swiftness and readiness to the movement of his life.

That movement was characterized by the most singular diligence. He was incapable of wasting time. What may have begun as a deliberately imposed rule of industry became a second nature to him. Not that it cramped him or withdrew him into the preoccupations of his work. He seemed able to transfer his whole attention at a moment's notice from one subject to another without any grinding of the gears of his mind. Interruption was powerless to fluster or apparently to irritate him. He covered in his stride day after day an immense range of detail. Apart from the regular work entailed by the administration of a growing Community, he was constantly engaged in correspondence with people in England and abroad who sought his advice on matters concerned with his special branches of learning. Each successive year saw some product of his study and research. Sermons, missions, retreats, lectures, numberless dealings with individuals all added to the fullness of his days. All moments spared from his immediate tasks were devoted to the endless marshalling of the minutiae of liturgical documents that provided the data for his published writings. He would speak lightly of

what to the layman seemed tedious drudgery. 'It satisfies the
interest which people find in a cross-word puzzle.' Even conversation or discussion would hardly arrest his industrious
activity. Nothing is more characteristic than the memory of
him cutting the leaves and skimming with a discriminating
eye over the pages of a learned periodical while others talked,
and then intervening in the argument with an incisive and
sometimes devastating comment: as when, in a pause after a
visitor had urged upon the company the thesis that all illness
was remediable and due to some defect in the faith of the
individual sufferer, Frere shot out the question: 'Is there any
respectable way of dying?' He seemed never too busy to take
on some fresh task—to write the music of a College play, or
a descant for a hymn in church: to hunt up some reference
required for someone else's work: or to prepare the outlines
of an office-book for a religious community.

The bow was rarely relaxed; he seldom took any exercise:
but sometimes he would sit down to the piano and play and
sing through the best part of a Wagner opera—or some
songs of Schubert or Hugo Wolf: and in this he found his
best *détente* and refreshment. But despite the toll he levied
upon his body there was apparent no strain of mind or spirit.
Everything about him was quick, light, clear and cool. No
confusion of mind or heat of spirit stayed his course.

If this diligence of industry marked his work, it was no
less conspicuous in the fashioning of his inward life. One may
only uncertainly surmise the heights to which the spires of
his prayer soared. What is certain is that they sprang out of a
fabric of devotion of great architectural elaboration and
strength. Into this fabric the Bible and the Church's liturgy
were deeply and intricately inwrought. His Hebrew Old
Testament and Greek New Testament display in their mark-
ings, annotations, and cross-references astonishing evidence
of the way in which he wove them into the texture of his
prayers. And the liturgical forms and patterns explored by
the scholar clothed with a living idiom the worship which
was the primary habit of his life. It has been said of literary

style that it is the man himself: and in nothing does Frere's
spirit reveal itself more evidently than in the style of his
prayer so far as he gave it outward expression. To hear him
conduct a prayer-meeting was to know a little what St. Paul
meant by the words, 'enriched in all utterance'. The very
spirit of prayerfulness seemed to utter itself upon a fine
instrument, each string of which was struck in turn. Nor was
it the less free and spontaneous because it was schooled in
the deeply-appropriated language of the Church's worship.
At the Edinburgh Conference of 1910 Frere was one of the
persons chosen to lead the whole assembly in prayer. A distinguished Presbyterian said afterwards that it was a revelation of what strength and depth could be given to extempore
prayer by a mind nourished and schooled by habituation in
the classical forms of liturgical worship. But, elaborately as
he employed Scripture and liturgy as the medium of devotion, the qualities which marked his spirit were simplicity,
directness, and penetration—the more notable because they
belonged to a mind naturally subtle and elusive. In his traffic
with the things of the world he could be paradoxical and
incalculable, and would display a technique of diplomacy and
finesse worthy of a Renaissance Cardinal. But in the things
of God he was utterly simple and direct. And he seemed to
move in them with a strange sureness of foot. The epithets
used of the spirit of divine Wisdom come to the mind as
descriptive of Walter Frere's spiritual quality: 'Quick of
understanding, holy, subtle, freely moving, clear in utterance.' No smoke obscured the light in him: the very detachment of his emotions served to enhance the clarity of his per-
ceptions. The truths of the Faith shone for him in their own
light and needed no elaborate apologia. When he spoke of
them it was in language exquisite indeed in its distinction,
but such as a child might understand; not because he was
condescending to smaller understandings than his own, but
because it seemed the truest and most natural way to speak
of the highest and deepest things. Those who sought his
spiritual direction know best how fresh and clear and bracing

was the light he threw upon the complexities of the soul. With one clean thrust he would probe the heart of the matter in a manner so trenchant as to make one wince: and then supply the remedial and encouraging counsel. In ordinary intercourse he gave to some an impression of aloofness and even of coldness. But in his ministry to individuals he displayed a deep solicitude and an inexhaustible patience. Those who sought him in trouble were met by a most winning tenderness that they could hardly have guessed at from his common demeanour. Indeed, it was a very delicate chivalry that impelled him to undertake the cause of those who had fallen by the way or who suffered from the world's obloquy. And it may safely be said that nothing characterized his prayer more markedly than the assiduity and range of his intercession—as the much-used copy of his own manual, *Sursum Corda*, eloquently testifies.

The authority that Walter Frere exercised in the Community was due as much to the eminence of his mind and spirit as to the prerogative of his office. The latter was defined in a special way in the Community of which he was so long Superior. It is a mistake to suppose that a religious community can be described adequately in terms of any secular polity. To be sure, theories of government prevalent at any given period find some reflexion in the life and institutions of the Church. And the liberal and democratic ideas astir at the time of the Community's formation doubtless contributed something to the colour of its constitution. But far more potent than the influence of any political analogy was the special ideal set before the Community of reproducing the life of the first Christians, of whom it is recorded that 'the multitude of them that believed were of one heart and soul'. It was in order that the whole body of the Community might learn to grow in a common mind by the difficult process of the mutual submission of all its members one to the other in the fear of Christ that the supreme authority within the Community is vested in its Chapter. In the deliberations and decisions of Chapter every professed brother is bidden

53

to take his full share of responsibility. And it is this same ideal which accounts, on the one hand, for the emphasis laid on respect for the individual's conscience and on the development of his particular faculty and, on the other hand, for the requirement that he should identify his will with that of the Community. The authority of the Superior is thus constitutionally limited. But within the limits it has a large area for its exercise and initiation. He is specially responsible for maintaining the observance of the Rule: all the work of the brethren is done under his direction and sanction: and he is the head of a Religious family the welfare of each member of which he is concerned to study and provide for. And, more generally, it belongs to his office to guide the policy and development of the Community.

Light as were his hands upon the reins and sparing as was his use of the imperative, there was no mistaking Frere's governing touch upon the life of the Community, composed as it was in those earlier days of men of forcible character and strongly-marked individuality. Sometimes he could give a sharp pull upon the curb, or by an incisive word check some incongruity. But in the main he used his authority to stimulate and give direction to the capacities of the brethren. He was more concerned to enlist their co-operation and to develop their initiative than to impose his orders. His control of Chapter was the more powerful because it was so unheavy-handed. The far-sighted clarity of his mind, his detachment from the pressure of excited feelings and from all self-importance, the flexibility of his adjustment to unexpected situations enabled him to give the lead through all perplexities. Incalculable he often was: it was difficult to predict what line he would take. For one thing, he was generally two moves ahead of anyone else, and when you thought to come up with him he was away and beyond. And in matters which fall short of ultimate principles he was not greatly careful of consistency.

He seemed sometimes to manipulate circumstances with an almost airy dexterity, and even with a certain roguish opportunism: and his unexpected turns would bewilder the plodding pedestrian trying to keep step with his rapid measure. To speak in the language of chess, he would seem to have preferred the knight's-move to any other, partly perhaps as a way to escape capture by partisans and their clichés. And sometimes he would use positively naughty dialectical devices in order, one surmised, to prevent an inadequate solution of a question from becoming hard-set, and to keep open the way for one that only his learning and foresight could discern. In such moments his own description of one of the Popes, 'A strange mixture of saintliness and foxiness', seemed not altogether inappropriate to himself. Undoubtedly there was an element in his conduct of life's business that eludes explanation. But his power to govern derived from the steely discipline with which he governed himself—a discipline clothed with so debonair a grace and gaiety as almost to conceal its moral greatness.

In the first year of Frere's Superiorship were begun the main corporate works in which, ever since, the Community has been engaged. To the inauguration of them he brought all his constructive resources and practical ingenuity. He was ready to take daring risks which the counsels of financial prudence would have discouraged. His impulse was to plan on large-scale dimensions. With that he had a remarkable capacity for improvisation and for utilizing such equipment, material and personal, as was available, despite its deficiencies. I think that for him mankind was divided into two classes only—the few of first-class ability and the rest. If the former were lacking, one must 'make do' with the latter. Certainly he could make terrifying demands upon the less-gifted: but he would lay open with lavish generosity his own resources for their assistance.

The first undertaking with which he was concerned was the foundation of the College for the training of ordinands. If the idea of throwing open a wider door of access to the Ministry, and at the same time of providing a more prolonged and thorough training for it than had been prevalent, did not originate with him, it was he above all who made it effectual. Buildings had to be adapted, tutors procured: affiliation of the College to the University of Leeds negotiated, a residentiary hostel at Leeds established: suspicious bishops appeased: lecture-courses planned and provided: students selected, their needs financed, their corporate life fostered. In all this Frere displayed his resourcefulness and dexterity. Nor was he content with mere supervision. His influence permeated the early life of the College. Perfect in arrangement and crystal-clear in expression, his own lectures illuminated as by brilliant shafts of a searchlight whole periods of historical or liturgical development. He took a personal interest in the students and was easily accessible to them. There was no one whom they quoted more often and to whose voice, gait and style of address they more frequently paid the affectionate tribute of mimicry. He frankly charmed them—all the more because he did not try to do so. Many will remember the walks he led over the moors on College holidays, and the adroitness with which, on one of them, he mollified the surliness of a gamekeeper fearful of disturbance to his grouse. Under his auspices much polyphonic singing by students was introduced into the services in the church. Undaunted by performers of unequal skill he rehearsed assiduously 'Offertoria' by Palestrina and Vittoria, darting from part to part himself in aid of the distressed in a voice which, truth to say, blended but ill with other voices. Books still remain of parts written in his own manuscript and of descants written by himself.

Simultaneously with the foundation of the College began the Community's missionary work in South Africa, and a little later St. John's College, Johannesburg was taken over—a school for European boys which over the next years was to grow to such majestic proportions. Important as these works have been in the history of the Community, Frere had little to do with their immediate conduct, though they entailed constant correspondence between him and the brethren in South Africa. Twice he visited the Community houses in

56

Africa as Superior. On one of the voyages he wrote the Commentary on the Community Rule which, though subsequent revisions of the Rule have made it in some details out of date, is still a store-house of spiritual wisdom, and is written with a distinction of style that of itself invites to meditation on its subjects. Frere's vision, always ranging wide, included the hope of the Community establishing itself in yet another continent. At one time India, at another Canada was in his consideration. To the latter of these he paid more than one visit: and some of his most successful missions were preached there. But the Community grew more slowly than his hope anticipated: and such expansions are yet to seek.

Meanwhile there was growing up around the Community a large body of people, many of whom were united in the keeping of a religious rule of life, and all of whom have given powerful support to the works of the Community. The purpose of this Fraternity of the Resurrection as defined by Frere was 'to re-inforce in its members the power of the risen life in all its intensity; that they may resist their natural tendency to sink to the level of dull average Christian faith and practice: that they may provoke one another to the highest aims and ideals: and that they may jointly offer themselves to our Lord, to be used by Him as salt and leaven, in whatever way He sees to be best'. Attainment has fallen short of this high ideal. Yet the ideal itself persists and seeks in the changed conditions of a later age for fresh expression. The preface to the Rule of the Fraternity entitled 'The Spirit of the Rule' is one of the best examples of Frere's style of writing concerning the things of the Spirit. Free from all harmonium-tones it rings like good metal, cleanly struck.

Another enterprise which Frere found time among his multifarious researches and writings to promote was the publication of a series of manuals dealing in a popular manner with different aspects of Christian faith and practice. The largest number of these *Mirfield Manuals* were written by

Father Paul Bull, who had a genius for this kind of writing. But Frere himself wrote several—on the Bible, the Prayer Book, the relation of Church and State, and three or four devotional ones. The appearance of these manuals was the occasion of an outburst of Protestant agitation which for several years attended the evangelistic efforts of the 'Mirfield Monks'. The Archbishop of Canterbury, at that time Visitor of the Community, became much perturbed; and Frere was involved in a long correspondence with him, in which he upheld the refusal of the Community to censor the publications and utterances of its members. The controversy reached a histrionic climax at a meeting in London on behalf of the Community's work at which the Archbishop courageously spoke, despite his alarms. A Protestant champion advanced menacingly and, brandishing his umbrella in the Archbishop's face, denounced him as a traitor. All this hubbub marked a turning-point in the relations of the Community to its own neighbourhood. Many in the West Riding had been puzzled about the nature of the 'House of the Resurrection' that had arisen overnight in one of its valleys. Fears were expressed that this 'House of Correction' would fall upon the rates. A variant interpretation was that a 'House of Recreation' had mysteriously been established at Mirfield. A visit of Mr. Kensit to Mirfield to denounce the Community at a public meeting gave its Superior the opportunity to address a crowded out-of-door gathering. Standing on a chair in front of the 'Black Bull', whence liquid refreshment was passed, as he spoke, to some of his nearest audience, he explained with equal frankness and good-humour the purpose of the Community and its manner of life. This speech, given wide circulation in the local newspapers, went far to create a new friendliness between the Community and its neighbours.

In another direction Frere's sympathies with the Labour Movement, more stridently expressed by other members of the Community, gave rise to the impression that it was identified with Socialism—still at that time a term of opprobrium.

Meetings with Labour leaders took place at Mirfield. The presence at one of these of Mr. Keir Hardie was regarded by some as marking a new era in the relations between the Church and Labour: by others as portending a sinister alliance. At another of such meetings in the Quarry in the Community grounds, Mrs. Pankhurst, the Suffragette leader, appeared uninvited and mysteriously contrived to ascend the speaker's rostrum, whence none of Fr. Frere's blandishments could induce her to descend until she had exhausted the torrent of her eloquent propaganda. Frere was not a deep student of Christian sociology: nor was he filled with the moral passion of the prophet. Still less was he liable to the sentimental Utopianism which clouds even while it kindles the minds of many would-be reformers. Nor was he a party-man. Instinctively he eluded capture by majorities and was restive if he found himself in one, as though he knew that the truth was unlikely to be found in its possession. But he had a strong impulse to identify himself with the 'under-dog' and the dispossessed.

All through the years up to the war of 1914 Frere took his full share in the mission work of the Community. He lacked some of the qualifications of a missioner. Penetrating and lucid as was his preaching, and appealing as it did to the more spiritually awake, it was hardly charged with sufficient emotional force to break through the defences of the somnolent and calloused. Congregations waiting to be blown out of their spiritual trenches by shell-fire were often unmoved by the thrusts of his keen rapier. Probably the best evangelistic work Frere did was in the years when he and Fr. Bull conducted missions together. No two men could be less alike in their technique. The flavour both of the matter and of the form of their preaching was as different as that of hot chocolate from a dry white wine. But together they achieved a combination of heat and light that had a high evangelistic efficacy.

It is impossible to record the multiplicity and variety of Frere's occupations during the years in the Community before he was made bishop.[1] But any such record would be misleading if it obscured the primacy that he gave to the practice of devotion and to the unfailing regularity of its exercises. Mass, Office, Meditation, Intercession—these no pressure of business was allowed to pretermit or postpone. And again, it is impossible to exaggerate the central place that he occupied in the family life of the Community. It was always touched with a new interest and zest when he was at home. It was not a matter of understanding or failing to do so, of agreeing or disagreeing. He could be enigmatic, paradoxical, provoking—yes, provoking. But there was a fascination about him—the greater because he was so little self-conscious and so detached. One constantly had one ear cocked to hear what he was saying. The very charm of his bodily presence, the dancing swing of his walk, the movement of his hands turning the leaves of a book, the grace and naturalness of his ceremonial acts—all these contributed to the impression he made. And they signified greater things.

The 'Gallic clarity' of his mind, his accessibility, his swift readiness to help, the pungency and gaiety of his spirit, the wasteless order of his life, his serenity and calm, his disciplined liberty, his freedom from pique and pettiness, the lightness with which he carried his learning, his indifference to ecclesiastical small-talk, his religious fidelity, and, penetrating all, his selflessness—these were the gifts which were the secrets of his authority and which so profoundly influenced the life of the Community.

[1] These included the charge of Serbian theological students at St. Stephen's House, Oxford (now demolished to make room for the new Bodleian annexe) during the first World War. In 1916 Frere had ceased for a time to be Superior, and so was able to take up his quarters at Oxford with Fr. Hallward as his companion and helper. The latter records his 'general impression that the venture was disappointing. Fr. Frere won the students' affections; they were grateful for the Oxford experience and for the hospitality which we gave them there. But I don't think that he established any *lasting* links with them and their Church. He was not to them what he was to the Russians.'

4

ELEVATION TO THE EPISCOPATE

by C. S. Phillips

For a considerable number of years before Frere was made a bishop members of the uninitiated clerical rank and file might have been heard discussing this as a possibility. It is unlikely, however, that any such step was even contemplated before the offer of Truro in 1923. Frere's reputation for 'very High Church views', and still more his association with a monastic community (in which he bore the un-Protestant-sounding title of 'Superior'), were hardly likely to commend him in the exalted quarters where such things are settled. Moreover, though his reputation stood high both in ecclesiastical and in learned circles, he at no time of his life attracted great attention from the general public. It may well have been thought, too, that if an offer were made it would be declined. Certainly, Gore had accepted a bishopric; but that was in 1901, when the Community of the Resurrection was hardly out of its experimental stage—very different from the large and stable institution which grew steadily year by year to maturity under his successor's fostering care.

An absurd story had been current when the Deanery of St. Paul's was vacant in 1911 after the death of Dr. Gregory. Nearly a generation later a priest taking temporary duty in the diocese of Truro, who had been assured at the time by certain people that they knew 'for a positive fact' that the post had been offered to Frere, summoned up courage to ask the Bishop if there was any truth in the story. The Bishop laughed. 'But you haven't finished it,' he said; 'it goes on to say that I answered "No" on the back of a postcard.' He added that the sole foundation for the story was that an influential friend had suggested his name to the Prime Minister.

The one offer that we know for certain to have been made was that of a canonry of Windsor in 1921. In regard to this the Rev. Dr. A. V. Baillie, who was Dean of Windsor at that time, furnishes the following note:

'I have always believed that the canons of Windsor should be specialists in some kind of learning, as canonries are an ideal platform from which to give expression to their knowledge. As a rule, though I pressed the general principle on the King, I did not think it right to suggest any particular name when there was a vacancy. But I made two exceptions. I pressed for Alexander Nairne, who came with infinite benefit to our community; and I pressed for Frere himself because of his liturgical scholarship. The King consented, though he did not like Frere's reputation for advanced views. The offer was made; but Frere felt he could not sever his connection with the Mirfield brotherhood. Of course, the case of a bishopric was different. As this is an old story now, I don't think there is any objection to making it public.'

Meanwhile the proposals for the revision of the Prayer Book which issued in the abortive 'Deposited Books' of 1927 and 1928 were making their dilatory way through the two Convocations and (later) the Church Assembly. In these proceedings Frere played a part that increased continually in importance, his official status being that of a representative of the diocese of Wakefield in the Lower House of York Convocation. He had been elected as such by the clergy of the archdeaconry of Halifax on 29th Jan. 1914—an election which, on 10th Feb. of the following year, the Archbishop of York (Dr. Lang), after a formal hearing of the case, accepted as valid notwithstanding the candidate's unbeneficed status. It was obvious from the start that Frere's expert knowledge

gave him a very special claim to be heard on liturgical matters; and he was to become more and more effective as a
counterpoise to the presence in the northern Upper House
at that time of a solid *bloc* of bishops, able, extremely vocal
and of advanced Protestant opinions,[1] whose attitude to the
whole business of revision was the reverse of sympathetic. In
two speeches on 24th Nov. 1915 he gave strong expression to
the view that the Communion Office should not be excluded
(as many desired) from the optional variants which it was at
that time proposed to embody in a Supplement or Appendix
to the Book of Common Prayer. He pointed out the dis-
satisfaction that was felt with the Office as it stood, and said
that 'every one knew, as a matter of fact, that from a liturgical
aspect their Service Book was the least satisfactory in Christendom.' He himself pleaded for 'a modest rearrangement',
with 'the insertion of words invoking the Holy Spirit in the
Prayer of Consecration'. This view was to prevail more and
more in both Convocations (apart from the Upper House of
York, where the *bloc* remained intransigent); and in Oct.
1918 the two archbishops were asked to call a special conference to discuss it. The conference produced an agreed
solution which was sponsored by the Evangelical Bishop
Drury of Ripon and the Anglo-Catholic Dr. Frere. This
proposed the moving back of the Prayer of Humble Access
to before the *Sursum Corda*, the insertion of a new section
containing an Anamnesis and an Invocation of the Holy
Spirit immediately after the Words of Institution, and the
placing of the Lord's Prayer (with introduction) at the end of
the Prayer of Consecration—the Prayer of Oblation being
kept in its old position after the Communion. The solution in
question was accepted by both Houses of Southern Convocation on 11th Feb. 1920; and on the same day was introduced into the Northern by Bishop Drury in the Upper and
by Frere in the Lower House. The latter speaker admitted
frankly that the solution was a compromise, but described it

[1] The Archbishop said that he sometimes felt as though he were taking the
chair at a meeting of the Church Association.

as 'a compromise of hope', for the other alternative, viz. 'at this stage to say, "We are powerless, we can do nothing, we cannot agree",' would be, he thought, 'a counsel of despair'. His pleading was successful; and the motion was passed by 34 votes to 29. But in the Upper House an amendment to reject the proposal was only defeated by the Archbishop's casting vote; and, even so, two amendments to its provisions were insisted on by a majority in each case. In consequence a Joint Meeting of both Houses was held on 29th April following, at which the conference's plan was rejected by 28 votes to 25. Apart from this the revision proposals, in the form which they had reached, were accepted by both Convocations.

These had now finished their stage of the proceedings, and the scene shifted to the newly erected Church Assembly. A committee of its three Houses, Bishops, Clergy and Laity, was appointed in the autumn of 1920 to report on what had been done by Convocation. Of this committee Frere was a member; and among his papers between the leaves of one of the innumerable pamphlets of the time a letter survives in which the chairman, Bishop Gibson of Gloucester (Frere's old Principal at Wells) writes, 'We need you badly'. The committee presented its report in June 1922, adopting the majority of the Convocations' proposals.

Of Frere's part in the debates that followed the Rev. Dr. J. H. Srawley, Canon and Chancellor of Lincoln Cathedral, who had much to do with those debates and with Frere personally, contributes the following appreciation:

'After general approval had been given to the Revised Prayer Book (Permissive Use) Measure (N.A. 84) by all three Houses (by the House of Clergy on 31st Jan. 1923) the next stage was its consideration by each of the Houses sitting separately. The first and only session of the House of Clergy in which Frere took part was on 2nd–6th July 1923. Before the next session (13th–15th Nov.) he had been elevated to the episcopate, and the House of Clergy had, to their loss, to do without his help.

'During this first set of sessions in July none of the more

contentious phases of revision had been reached. The House was confronted with a variety of alternatives to particular sections of N.A. 84, e.g. the E.C.U. proposals in the Green Book, the Life and Liberty Movement proposals in the Grey Book. Frere shewed himself ready to allow a large liberty, disconcerting to some members, in the way of varieties, but was insistent that the proper liturgical sequence of the Offices of Mattins and Evensong should be kept, beginning with "O Lord, open thou our lips", except that, when Holy Communion followed, the Office might end with *Benedictus*. In the debates he shewed the same sprightly debonair manner with which we were all familiar, often surprising partisans of various schools by his independence of judgment and a certain subtlety of thought which passed their comprehension, together with delightful flashes of humour.

'He acted during that July session for the members in charge of the Measure, and introduced many of the proposals, and, of course, his prestige and wide liturgical knowledge always won the attention of the House, though (as I have said) he surprised them sometimes by his *tours de force*. The discussions at this earlier session were largely provisional and members were feeling their way. That, I imagine, is why Frere was willing to acquiesce in such a large liberty of variations in the sections dealing with the Daily Offices, Litany, etc. The contentious questions of the Holy Communion Service, Reservation, etc., had not been reached when he ceased to be a member of the House of Clergy.

'Of course, he played a large part in the compiling of the Orange Book, eventually embodied in the three Alcuin Club Books, *A Survey of the Proposals for the Alternative Prayer Books*, Pts. i, ii, iii, forming a third in the triad of what was described by the Chairman, Dean Ryle, as the "rainbow literature". And his object in these surveys was to reconcile and bring together all that was best in each of them. Here, again, he shewed considerable ingenuity and subtlety.'

Frere's learning, tact and persuasiveness as shewn in these protracted discussions won admiration on all sides and made

E

him much better known in official Church circles than he had been before. To a quite exceptional degree he had succeeded in disarming the suspicion and distrust with which those of his way of thinking are normally regarded by the majority of their fellow-Churchmen. So at least thought Archbishop Davidson, who was moved to take the bold step of pressing both the Prime Minister (Mr. Baldwin) and Frere himself to consider the latter's elevation to the see of Truro, which had become vacant through the translation of Dr. Guy Warman to Chelmsford.

The Archbishop's views and motives are clearly set out in a letter which he wrote to Frere on 28th Aug. 1923. The letter has been printed by the Bishop of Chichester in his biography of Archbishop Davidson; and the most important paragraph in it is here reproduced with the Bishop of Chichester's kind permission:

'It is not lightly that I have pressed upon the Prime Minister the conclusion I have reached after quiet consultation with Ebor, with Winton and with others. For a long time past I have felt strongly that the Church had been suffering from the fact that there was no one who could speak with responsibility on behalf of what is called, however inadequately, Anglo-Catholicism, and yet be able to regard these questions largely, sanely and with the equipment of scholarly knowledge. Men who can do this can certainly be found. But that is not enough. We need someone whom the Prime Minister can fairly be urged to nominate, as a man who carries the confidence of Churchmen generally, whether they are of his school or not. It would be both futile and unfair were I to urge the Prime Minister to nominate to the episcopate some admirable men whose virtues and capacities I myself know, but who would be neither known nor trusted by the rank and file of Churchmen of all schools. There is one man who does possess the qualifications which—when I think it all out before God—seem to me to be essential, and you are the man. This is no fad of mine, as you know well. It is the view, so far as I can judge, of all whom you would specially trust or who have a special claim on your attention. I have acted with a deep conviction in what I have done, and I unhesitatingly believe that I am right.'[1]

Such words were not only pleasant to hear, coming from such a source, but also touching and full of sound sense. At first, however, Frere refused to fall in with the proposal. For many centuries *nolo episcopari* has been one of the stock jokes of the cynic; but there can be no doubt that Frere's refusal and his motives for it were utterly sincere. He had been wedded for over thirty years to his Community and to the 'religious' life; and he had no desire and saw no necessity to change his state. Also he felt himself too old. '*Why*', he asked Fr. Horner after his appointment, 'do they want to send me there at this age?' But the Archbishop was determined and persistent, and after further correspondence a way was found in the end of making it possible for Frere to become Bishop of Truro without ceasing to be a full member of his Community. This removed the one otherwise insuperable obstacle. Frere accepted, and the appointment was announced. His consecration followed at Westminster Abbey on All Saints' Day (1st Nov.), 1923.

Among the letters of congratulation he received was one from Robert Bridges, who wrote (14th Oct): 'The Chilswell party send you their love and congratulations on your appointment—which surprised me in so far as I never heard of so "extreme" a "high ch. man" being so favoured. I am sure that you will like it.' Another from Bishop Talbot of Winchester ran: '. . . Bless you! Ted has suggested that you might like my little simple ebony and silver staff—given me by Leeds Clerical Club—which has done most of my work in South London and in Winchester. I used to carry it about myself as Tram Bishop like a banjo in its green baize.' The offer was gratefully accepted and the staff in use throughout Frere's episcopate.

A full account of Frere's life and work as Bishop of Truro by two closely connected with him is given in the next chap-

[1] Bell, *Life of Randall Davidson*, (1 vol. ed.), pp. 1250-1.

ter. But, especially in these days, a bishop's activity is by no means confined to diocesan work. It is necessary that he should also play his part in the central councils of the Church; and, with the question of Prayer Book revision reaching its climax, these were bound to make even greater demands than usual, and on Frere especially in view of his exceptional equipment. We have the authority of a bishop who is specially qualified to know for saying that 'he was at once so clearly convinced and so transparently sincere that he won general approval and the respect of his brethren. The most notable instance was his devotion to the new Canon. He was convinced that it was securely grounded in the best liturgical tradition, and when the Archbishop of York' [then Dr. Lang] 'pressed the claims of those who desired a mere shifting of the Prayer of Oblation Frere opposed it again and again and carried most of the bishops with him. When he came to the bishops fresh from his splendid work in the House of Clergy, he was always fair and generous, and yet so clear and learned in regard to his own convictions, that in the early days he was a great help to the bishops as a whole.' Another bishop writes: 'You could not help feeling that he was both the saint and the scholar in everything he did or said. He was also an artist. All these three elements combined and gave him a rare quality and a very rare distinction. There was an otherworldliness about him which detached him from too great an absorption in the actual business of administration, though he did everything most patiently and carefully. . . . I have always understood that he was particularly conciliatory in everything concerning the Prayer Book, though I suppose that he ran the 1928 Canon rather hard. . . . In all the debates at Convocation in which he intervened he had something to say. He never wasted time. He was never ponderous.'

From all this it is clear that Frere's influence with his brother-bishops was even exceptionally strong at first. But there seems reason to believe that it considerably declined later. He had always a tendency towards the paradoxical and unexpected; and this appears to have grown on him. Possibly (as a brother-bishop has suggested) 'he disliked the whole process of having to commend his views to anyone else who did not really agree with him, and so developed a kind of nonchalant, Puckish mode of doing so.' The result was to win for him in some quarters a reputation for 'airiness' and lack of actuality. This may have been due in part to the quality of 'otherworldliness' noted above. It is quite possible, too, that as he grew old he found ecclesiastical politics and many of the questions with which bishops in council are compelled to deal increasingly uncongenial and even boring. He certainly seemed to grow less and less 'clerical' in his outlook and tastes: the musician (or so one suspected) more and more came to the surface—and musicians are always a race apart. He once startled a Sunday luncheon table at Lambeth by saying, 'I think we are always trying to give people more religion than they want' (he was maybe going off to a Sunday afternoon concert at the Albert Hall). Should it perhaps be added that after being Superior of a monastic community for nearly twenty years he may not have found it altogether easy to be a single voice among many? There was always a touch of the autocrat about him—a trait against which he indubitably struggled, but not to be entirely eliminated. It was 'the defect of the quality' of a very strong man.

If, however, Frere's influence in matters of general policy was slight in the last years of his episcopate, his fellow-bishops both at home and abroad were at all times more than willing to pick his brains on particular points, especially those relating to historical and doctrinal matters. The Archbishop of Canterbury writes to him for information about episcopal signatures, the Archbishop of Dublin about pectoral crosses, several bishops about pontifical ceremonial, the Bishop of Bombay about bishops' thrones; while his old Trinity and Wells friend, Frank Norris, Bishop in North China, brings to him a knotty problem about a Russian 'lady of mature age' at Tientsin who wishes to be recognized as an Anglican from possibly other than purely religious motives. His answers to these varied queries shew the extraordinary range of his knowledge, and a selection of them might well be published some day.

In one branch of an English diocesan's duties Frere (as might perhaps have been expected) took little part. His turn to enter the House of Lords did not arrive till 1930; and when it did he never spoke there. Characteristically, he failed to inform the members of his family beforehand of the date of his introduction. Later in the same afternoon he arrived at his sister's flat and was asked where he had been. He replied, 'I've just been introduced into the House of Lords'; and the ensuing cries of, 'Why on earth didn't you let us know?' seemed to cause him genuine surprise.

This seems to be a convenient place for a brief review of some of Frere's other extra-diocesan activities during his episcopate which cannot easily be fitted in elsewhere.

1. Frere's share in the one Lambeth Conference during his episcopate, that of 1930, was cut short by the state of his health. (Shortly before, the breaking of a blood-vessel over one eye one Sunday morning in Truro Cathedral had marked the beginning of the gradual failure of his physical powers in his last years.) The following letter to Archbishop Lang offers his apologies:

'I send just a line to report that I have come from the Conference with many regrets that my health doesn't hold out enough for me to continue to the end. In fact, I have been able to do more than I undertook at the beginning—namely, not only to sit on Committees, but to follow our discussions on Committees' reports. But more than that I couldn't well do; and, as it was, there were one or two little signs that instead of getting mended I was beginning to go back a bit—so forgive my flight. .... I am trying to follow it the best I can from a distance and not to mind too much being out of it all in this way.'

2. The subject of religious communities was one in regard to which Frere's unique position and experience gave him a special authority both with his brother-bishops and with the communities themselves. The Ven. Guy Hockley, Archdeacon of Cornwall, writes as follows:

'One of the most significant results of the Oxford Movement has been the revival in the Church of England of the Religious Life under the threefold vows. During the past hundred years a large number of communities, both contemplative and active, for men and women, have been founded. In general they have been regarded with friendly tolerance or approval by the bishops; and in most cases the bishop of the diocese where they established themselves was invited to be their Visitor. But they organized themselves on their own independent lines, and had no official recognition or sanction from the rulers of the Church as a body. This was probably the wisest—possibly the only—method practicable in the early days of the Movement, but it was not ideal or satisfactory as a permanent situation. In course of time, as was inevitable, complications occurred, and difficult problems of ecclesiastical discipline, constitution, order and practical administration presented themselves. It became increasingly evident that the time was overdue for the whole position to be considered and the status of the communities and their relation to the episcopate adjusted and regularized. In accordance with the suggestions made by a committee of the Lambeth Conference of 1930, and after careful and friendly consultations between the bishops and representatives of the communities, an advisory council was formed for the purpose of ordering the relations of bishops and religious communities, and regulations for the guidance of its work were drawn up. In directing this important scheme in accordance with wise and well-considered principles, and in the conduct of the prolonged negotiations which preceded it, Frere's historical knowledge, intimate personal experience of the Religious Life, and sound judgment, were of incalculable service.'

3. Concerning the most important of Frere's extra-diocesan activities as Bishop of Truro (apart from his contribution to the Lambeth discussions on the Revised Prayer Book)—viz. his share in the Malines Conversations between representatives of the Anglican and Roman Catholic Churches respectively at intervals between 1921 and 1926— we may be excused from saying much here, as he himself told the story of the Conversations in a series of articles in the *Truro Diocesan Gazette*, which were later published in book form. To this engaging little volume, *Recollections of Malines*, the reader is referred, along with the official Report of the Conversations and the relevant chapters in the Bishop of Chichester's life of Archbishop Davidson. It must suffice to jot down a few bare facts, with the names of those who participated.

The first stages of the Conversations took place before Frere became a bishop. They originated quite unofficially in 'some talk' between Viscount Halifax and Cardinal Mercier, Archbishop of Malines, in October 1921. On his return Lord Halifax immediately approached Frere (at all times a specially intimate and trusted friend), and it was as the result of consultation between the two that the Dean of Wells, Dr. Armitage Robinson, was chosen to be the third Anglican representative at the First Conversation, which took place at Malines on 6th–8th Dec. 1921, with the Cardinal, Abbé Portal and Mgr Van Roey, the Cardinal's Vicar-General, representing the other side. The Second Conversation was held on 14th, 15th March 1923, when the same representatives took part. It should be noted that it was in the following July that Frere made his public and much publicized protest against the telegram of greeting sent by the 1923 Anglo-Catholic Congress to the Pope. The Anglican authorities (who, of course, were in touch throughout with what was being done) had begun to shew themselves rather nervous about the Conversations; and the telegram seemed likely to make things worse. However, it was decided to go on; and a Third Conversation was fixed for 7th, 8th Nov. of the same year—

which (as it happened) was a week after Frere's consecration as bishop. It had by this time come to be felt that the really crucial question of Papal Supremacy must be specifically and roundly tackled, and that the number of representatives on both sides should be increased. Bishop Gore and Dr. Kidd, Warden of Keble, were therefore brought in on the Anglican side, and Mgr Batiffol and Père Hemmer to balance them on the Roman. The participants were the same at the Fourth Conversation (19th, 20th May 1925). A further conversation fixed for 25th Jan. 1926 had to be postponed through what proved to be the Cardinal's last illness; and the Fifth Conversation did not take place till 11th Oct. 1926. At this Mgr Van Roey, Mercier's successor at Malines, presided over a reduced gathering—Abbé Portal being dead and Bishop Gore and the Dean of Wells absent; and in the circumstances it was felt that all that was possible was the drafting of an interim report concerning what had been done so far. This, after a good deal of delay, was published (Jan. 1928) as a pamphlet in French and English, *The Conversations at Malines*. But by that time the wind at the Vatican had veered to the north—and so matters could go no further. Probably it was only the charity, enthusiasm and unique prestige of the great Cardinal that had made it possible for them to go as far as they did.[1]

With reference to the part played by Frere (and others) in these happenings Dr. Kidd has contributed the following note:

'I suppose that the leaders on our side were Bishop Gore, Dean Armitage Robinson and Bishop Frere. Each of them, I think, made his peculiar contribution to the result, and also made his personal impression; for, besides the formal discussions, there was much done towards mutual understanding in the happy intercourse of conversation, at meals for

[1] Visitors to Lis Escop will remember the large inscribed photograph of Cardinal Mercier (now at Mirfield) which hung to the right of the mantel-piece in the hall, representing him sitting on his throne in all the glory of full archiepiscopal paraphernalia, including the pallium and the gorgeously embroidered *gremiale* covering the knees.

instance, or one to another at other times. I think Gore was less elastic in mind than the other two: he had reached his conclusions and stood firm; so, when some point of importance arose he was apt to sound rather unyielding. He and Batiffol, for instance, fell out over the amount of authority to be attached to the Vincentian maxim:[1] Gore affirmed and Batiffol declined it—and that was that. Nevertheless, Gore carried great weight. The Dean, I remember, in some discussion about the relation between St. Peter and the other apostles that arose out of the Epistle to the Ephesians managed to find points of agreement with the other side, but kept strictly within scriptural lines; and, in so doing, what he said on that and on other occasions sounded, and was, conciliatory. This was helped by his humorous way of talking: it made a special appeal to Cardinal Mercier; and they were great friends. Frere had all the gifts of learning and scholarship that either of them had; and they were reinforced by his extraordinary versatility and quickness of apprehension. It was he who kept the debates going, and yet safe. Moreover, his industry was astounding. He kept elaborate notes as the discussion was proceeding, and yet was able to attend to what was said; and from these notes he wrote up his *Recollections*, and also, day by day, acting as joint secretary with Père Hemmer, made a draft each evening of the report to be read over at the public session next morning. Looking back to what happened day by day, I think that his influence was greatest. This was partly due to his speaking French so easily. To hear Gore rolling it out, and then to hear him followed in the same tongue by Frere, was most amusing. But his personality told, even more than his gifts: and his "ways", which you know quite well, won everyone. We were treated as their friends, and equals; and each of us felt at home, and knew that he had the confidence of the rest. If Cardinal Mercier had not died, just before we were getting to the

[1] I.e. *Quod semper, quod ubique, quod ab omnibus*—the famous phrase used by Vincent of Lerins in his *Commonitorium* (434) to express the argument from universal consent.

fundamental difference—Papal Jurisdiction—I think we should have got much nearer to one another. Nevertheless, I hope the results will appear in time; and I believe that Frere, on our side, had the largest share in promoting them.'

4. Less known to Church circles in general than Frere's share in the Malines Conversations was his work in connexion with the other great branch of Catholic Christendom —the Orthodox Church of the East, and in particular the Russian Church. Yet no side of his activity was more important or pursued with greater enthusiasm than this. Further, it is a side of which he himself has left no record (as he did of Malines), nor is a record easy to come by from any other quarter. For these reasons it seems fitting that it should be given a separate chapter later in this book, from the pen most competent to write it.

5

TRURO

by the late Ven. Guy W. Hockley, Archdeacon of Cornwall, and Prebendary W. R. Johnson, Rector of St. Ervan

'Walter Frere, Bishop of Truro! Well, I hope and believe he will make a very good, because a supernaturally-minded one.'—Von Hügel, *Letters to a Niece*, p. 197.

Elsewhere in this volume are described the gifts and contribution which Walter Frere brought to the Church at large as liturgiologist, historian, counsellor and, not least, as reconciler at Malines, and also his life as a Religious, with its provision of the environment, discipline and detachment which enabled him, beyond the fortune of most men, to offer those gifts and fulfil that contribution. In 1923, when he was in his sixtieth year, the opportunity was thrust upon him of working out the principles of ministry on which he had based himself and of showing how the fruits of devotion and learning could serve ordinary diocesan life. His episcopate was the unfolding of an idea and the realization of an ideal of a chief pastor's office in the Church.

What were the characteristics of the diocese, at the extreme south-west of England, to which he was called?

The diocese of Truro was, of course, a part of the ancient Exeter, which was, as the see city, in its turn the successor of Crediton, into which the bishopric of the Cornish had been merged in the tenth century. The diocese includes the whole

of Cornwall and the Scilly Isles, but it is not precisely co-
terminous with Cornwall, inasmuch as four parishes of
Devon come within the jurisdiction. It retains, as in its archdeaconry of Cornwall, in its method of appointment of deans
rural by election in the chapters, and in its Bishop Phillpotts'
Library at Truro, effects of that history. Across the penin-
sula, narrowing to the west, access is easy from sea to sea.
The terrible rocks of the coast guard it from the furious
breakers which its visitors know only if they come in winter.
The tempest blows over the high moors that protect the
fertile valleys, each with its little river, the deep lanes hung
with ferns, and the rich exotic gardens. Its industries are not
within factories: granite workings, the slate quarry at Delabole, the pyramids of slag from the china clay, shafts of
mines mostly derelict, and fishing boats—these are what
visitors see as the trains pass through a land that may strike
them as gaunt after Devon. From the height of the viaduct
that carries the Great Western Railway line into Truro the
traveller looks down upon the city in the basin of the hills.
It is all below him except, in the midst of the city, the
cathedral church. That seems to rise to his level, its towers
soaring over the dwellings of men to be part of the scene of
fields and woods beyond them. To such a traveller the
cathedral is symbolic of the claim of the Faith and of the
dominance of the Church: and when he hears that it has
come into being within the last seventy years he regards it as
the expression of a vigorous religious life. He is right. That
cathedral is the product of an age of faith. It was built—it is
not yet completed—by a generation of devoted church-
people, who looked forward to a Church of the far west, to
have its special mission to the Cornish people.

The future of the diocese of Truro was shaped by its first
two bishops, Dr. Benson and Dr. Wilkinson. Benson laid the
lines of both cathedral and diocese, closely modelled on those
of Lincoln, with which he had become familiar as canon
residentiary and chancellor of Lincoln Cathedral. The constitution of the cathedral body followed from his conception

77

of cathedral function. The symbolism worked out in the building is significant of those elements of history and interest which to his mind had to be perpetuated in stone and structure. Most cathedrals have grown, with adaptation to successive needs and with the offering of the wealth of successive generations; Truro sprang as one whole from its founders. It is a monument of a conception and of Cornwall.

Nor was the influence of Wilkinson less in the spiritual sphere. Truro has been from the beginning a diocese of definite churchmanship of a high Prayer Book standard. Probably no other in England has been more level, and the extremes of partisanship found elsewhere have been isolated eccentricities in Cornwall. It is difficult for those who have not been brought up in the heart of its Church life, but have come from ecclesiastical experience in other parts, to realize how they must abandon their expectations of party difference.

They must moreover be prepared for one extraordinary divergence from previous experience. They will soon find it in the permeating influence of Methodism. In the eighteenth century the Celtic temperament of the Cornish reacted with emotion to the preaching of Wesley, and, as if in an unloosing of psychical forces, developed the opportunity which was afforded to it by his doctrine of conversion. The Welsh, the other great branch of the Brythonic Celts, have exhibited a similar effect. Both in Wales and Cornwall astonishing tales are told of a mass-hysteria which is more interesting to the psychologist than it was approved by Wesley, and there were two further consequences. The Celtic character combined rigidity in some respects—as the selective and prohibitive observance of Sunday—with something like antinomianism in others. And the Methodist system became crystallized into almost the official Cornish religion. In our day it has practically discarded revivalism. It is no longer eccentric and racy. It has no longer the intensity which made details of organization so important as to lead in the earlier part of the nineteenth century to dissidence within Methodism itself. But still, as in most matters in Cornwall so in religion, the test is subjective: interest is in persons rather than in principles; what counts is feeling more than reason. The worship of the Church seems strange to it, of the Church's constitution and history it knows nothing, nor has the Church's claim to be the Body of Christ ever been rightly understood or penetrated its self-satisfaction. What animates it is the vague ethicism of a kindly people, who find in it an emotional outlet regulated by custom, and having now a century and a half of religious experience; in vitality thin, but in conservative inertia strong. The Cornish are certainly not stupid, but they suffer from certain limitations. The isolation of the Duchy, the highway to nowhere, is some explanation. Nor, when Cornwall became a holiday resort, did that tend to the best kind of change.

Church life in Cornwall, expressed in the revival of the see, was independent of this background, yet could not but be affected by it. In Ireland, where Rome is so strongly on the scene, the Church of Ireland reacts with Protestant sympathies; in Cornwall the reaction in the presence of Mthoedism has been towards a churchmanship specially sober, quiet and definite—three epithets inapplicable to the prevailing religiosity. This policy, for policy it unintentionally was, has been effective. It has, taking a broad view, saved the Church from permeation by the environment. It has given it cohesion, it has provided the ground for the development of its devotional genius, and it has attracted back that religious interest which was unsatisfied by emotionalism and a narrow piety. Yet there has not been much bitterness of antagonism. The chapel might regard the church as a place where salvation was doubtful, and church-people as uncertainly in the way of it because they made no point of emotional experience. Chapel might also work as a clique when elections were held and officials appointed. And church, though rather conscious of all that, went steadily on its way. But neither church nor chapel declined to lend to the other a farm-cart. The Jews had dealings with the Samaritans.

WALTER HOWARD FRERE

Into such an environment came Walter Howard Frere, the Mirfield monk, as those who wished to raise prejudice against him began to call him from the announcement of his appointment, and as he tranquilly and deliberately remained to his life's end. Archbishop Davidson's letter (printed in the last chapter) shews clearly his desire to secure Frere as a bishop. What it does not indicate is whether he intended to introduce, or at any rate guessed that he was introducing, a type and standard of episcopacy which had disappeared from the English Church, though known in the Anglican Communion elsewhere. The nearest parallel that comes to mind is that of Chinnery-Haldane, Bishop of Argyll and the Isles, in the last century. There have been in England and Wales many good bishops during four hundred years, and some not so good: there have been pastors, scholars, saints, confessors, martyrs. But the domestic background to their lives, whether or not they were married men, has been that of the household of the upper class. The very homes in which they live seem to expect that this should be so. Of course, strictly speaking, wherever the bishop lives, even if it be a cottage, is *palatium* as the residence of the chief spiritual officer. Into these palaces, sometimes castles, of the bishops of England, frequently palatial in other than the official sense, the bishops have imported the domesticity of their humbler days, enlarged to meet the new circumstances.

But with Frere this was not so. He carried his monastery with him wherever he went. He remained a full member of the Community of the Resurrection. He might on consecration have sought release from his vows, following the example of Dr. Gore, but he seems never to have contemplated such a step. If, reluctantly, he accepted a bishopric, he must be taken as he was. For the first time for four centuries a monk became, deliberately and with the knowledge of the Anglican authorities remaining a monk, a bishop of the English Church. 'I saw Walter Frere—for the first time as Bishop—as simple and as unspoilt as ever. What a good plan that is by which he remains a member of his fine Community, and, if and when he retires, finds his place there as before.'[1]

The home of the bishops of Truro—except Dr. Gott, who preferred to live at some distance from the city—is Lis Escop. Here a branch of the Community of the Resurrection was established and a company of the brethren—seldom less than three—lived with the Bishop. He and they retained the habit, customs and discipline of the Community. A small staff of servants assisted in the household work, which was of course out of proportion to what the brethren could undertake alone. In the chapel the Divine Office was said and the Chapter Mass daily celebrated.

Two members of the Community lived permanently at Lis Escop with the Bishop. Father King acted as his chaplain, and both he and Father Longridge found many opportunities of spiritual work in the diocese, such as sermons, lectures, retreats and quiet days. Dr. Mounsey, also of the Community, and formerly Bishop of Labuan and Sarawak, received a commission from the Bishop for work in the diocese as early as the autumn of 1925: and in 1930 was definitely appointed Assistant Bishop. He was not in continuous residence, but from the first paid occasional visits, which, as time went on, became more frequent and prolonged. Latterly, it meant that he was in Cornwall for the greater part of each year. He not only relieved the Diocesan Bishop of a large part of the work of confirmations, but was able to give valuable help in many other ways.

Mention should also be made of two others, who in their different ways did much to ease the burden of the Bishop's daily work. His secretary, Mr. Oswald Swete, was most efficient in dealing with correspondence, and keeping letters and other diocesan documents in businesslike order. Also his previous training and experience as an electrical engineer was of constant value in practical details of domestic needs, and in avoiding unnecessary expenditure.

Another friend and helper was his chauffeur. The Bishop

---

[1] Von Hügel, *Selected Letters*, p. 369.

had inherited from his predecessor both his car and his chauffeur, who became a well-known figure in the diocese. His good nature and ready humour secured him a welcome in the parsonages which they visited. His admiration and affection for the Bishop was unbounded, and at the Bishop's resignation he received from him a characteristic note of affectionate regard, of which he was justly proud.

The Bishop's mode of life at Lis Escop was the outward sign of the spirit of the episcopate. It was, so to say, episcopacy pure and simple. Yet the episcopate of the monk was not a mere reversion to what the episcopates of bishops drawn from the monastic orders had been before the Reformation. Walter Frere was too good a historian, too good a liturgiologist, too much of the twentieth century, to be imitatively medieval. He remained of his Community in the setting and ordering of his life; but he was entirely a bishop, and entirely Bishop of Truro, in this new work, as indeed he had always been entirely and independently himself in his interests and activities. He knew what episcopacy in fact has been in the history of the Church; he knew what it is in principle as a divine institution: with the lessons of the one to guide him and the inspiration of the other to embolden him he sought to make his diocese the scene of an episcopal administration as it should be, loving, pastoral, teaching, admonishing, and leading the flock to devotion and worship.

A particularly prominent place in the administration of a Bishop of Truro results from his relation to the cathedral church of the Blessed Virgin Mary. Truro is one of the few dioceses where the bishop is dean, and the arrangement gives an unusual opportunity to a bishop who is, as Benson was, liturgically minded. That the opportunity came also to the author of *The Principles of Religious Ceremonial* was singularly in the right nature of things. Frere, without being autocratic, made the most of it, and had as associates in the residentiary chapter a group of like-minded canons. The opportunity resembled that of which Dr. Scott Holland speaks in connexion with the appointment of Dr. Church to the Deanery of St. Paul's.[1]

It is worth while to dwell on this, for in Truro was gradually achieved a perfection of the English Rite, with its positive excellencies given their full value, its defects as far as might be supplemented, its proportion maintained, by an interpretation of it in its true spirit as one of the liturgies of the Catholic Church, and with that austere richness of ceremonial of which it admits.

The Eucharist is sung in the cathedral every Sunday and on festivals. The Bishop took great interest in the reverent and correct ordering of the ceremonial; and shortly before his resignation he issued a full and valuable directory for this purpose. In the preface to this he writes: 'In these few pages there is set down briefly what a six or seven years' experience of the Communion Service, authorized in 1928, has taught the clergy of Truro Cathedral as to the ceremonial details which a simple performance of that rite by three Sacred Ministers and their attendants, is found to involve. A more elaborate ceremonial—as when incense is used, or when a bishop is either present or himself officiating—develops naturally, when required, out of the scheme as it is here set down.'

Upon the appointment of Frere to Truro, the English Church Union expressed their desire to offer him some gift, to mark his great services to the Union, and to the Catholic cause. In the event, this took the form of a substantial sum of money, which was placed at his disposal for any purpose which he should determine. The Bishop decided to use it to equip an additional chapel, at the extreme north-west of the cathedral: the decoration was entrusted to Mrs. Walke, a sensitive local artist, and it includes a painted reredos, of a remarkable and somewhat startling design, the central panel containing the Figure of Christ, in alb and girdle, surrounded by scenes depicting characteristic Cornish industries. The chapel—to be known as the Jesus Chapel—was

---

[1] *Life and Letters of Dean Church,* p. 258.

completed and dedicated in 1926: and the following inscription has been placed on the southern side of the screen which encloses it: 'The gift of the English Church Union to Walter Bishop of Truro at his consecration, All Saints' Day, 1923.'

Connected with the cathedral administration were two innovations. One was the distinction of the capes to be worn by the members of the chapter. They are blue, the colour associated with the Blessed Virgin Mary. Blue, it may be noted, has always been the colour of the cathedral school. These capes are worn by the residentiary and honorary canons in the offices in the parish churches as well as in the cathedral. They were welcomed by the diocese as a suitable and acceptable symbol.

The other new departure was the erection of an altar in the nave. This nave altar usually stands in its place, though it is movable and can be taken away to give space for the great diocesan assemblies. And it has the further value that it is a memorial to Winfrid Burrows—a bishop who seemed never to receive either in Truro or elsewhere the recognition due to his powers.

Of the occasional services in the cathedral two must be specially mentioned—the ordinations and the synods. With the synods a later part of this record deals, but something may be said here about the conduct of an ordination. In the diocese of Truro there are no large towns. The arrangement by which some priests would be trained in towns for town work and others in rural parishes for that of the countryside is mooted in the councils of the Church, but is not yet in being. Just as elementary education has throughout had a town bias (and is only now beginning to adapt itself in the country to the country), so the training of the clergy is almost entirely where the population is massed, not to say congested. The parishes of the west of England are mainly rural, or—except in the case of Exeter and Plymouth—of towns which run out into a connexion with the country and belong to deaneries which include country parishes. Most of them are parishes of one priest, and the incumbent when he needs a colleague usually does so in circumstances which require a priest and not a deacon. At no time therefore are there in Truro more than a few candidates for the diaconate. During Dr. Frere's episcopate some candidates, attracted by the distinction of the bishop, made a special effort to seek ordination in his diocese. He always held his ordinations at 8 o'clock, with the traditional ceremonial belonging to the rite: and those who have been ordained by him, as well as the worshippers at the Sunday Eucharist, will testify to the beauty, simplicity and dignity of the service.

In connexion with the ordination candidates the Guild of the Forerunner is to be remembered. The Guild (formed in 1926) was placed in the care of a warden appointed by the bishop, and membership was open to those, of not less than sixteen years of age, who hoped to be ordained whether in the diocese of Truro or elsewhere. Members were given a simple Rule of Life, and meetings were held twice a year for devotional, social and business purposes. From time to time retreats or quiet afternoons were arranged.

If the Bishop was thus concerned for the training of the ordination candidates, though their number was small (but he never regarded number), he was also greatly interested in the work of the Diocesan Training College. It was a Women's College—*was*, for the educational policy of the Church Assembly suppressed it in 1937; the last students were sent out to their work in July of the following year.

At the Training College it was felt very much that he was the bishop, not only in his diocesan capacity, but as chairman of the Council and, above all, as the friend of staff and students. As chairman, he presided over Council meetings at a very critical time in the history of the College. Difficult and delicate matters had to be decided, especially the relationship between Truro Training College and University College, Exeter, and St. Luke's College, Exeter, when all three united to form the 'South West Board' for the examination of teachers. It says much for his diplomacy that Truro Training

College, the smallest of the three, was allowed to make a full and useful contribution to all matters dealt with by the South West Board.

While the staff and students of the College welcomed Dr. Frere at public functions, they were even more glad to see him when he came to services in the College chapel or to the Whitsuntide reunions. Year by year he held a confirmation in the chapel. On one occasion after the service a student said, 'He is always so simple,'—then, as a great discovery— 'but there is always something to think about afterwards.' From time to time he said Mass for them, and always on Whitsunday. The chapel was dedicated to the Holy Spirit, and Whitsuntide was the college festival to which old students came back. One young sacristan said on a Whitsunday, 'He does love saying Mass.' In him the students were conscious of a spirituality which to some was a revelation.

When the Training College went the diocese lost an institution which not only provided mistresses largely for the elementary schools, provided and non-provided, of Cornwall, but also brought the diocese and the outside world together in the current of its influence. The Community of the Epiphany, of which the same might be said, remains.

This Community had its beginnings at St. Peter's, Eaton Square, in 1880, when George Howard Wilkinson was vicar, and moved with him to Truro. It has grown exceedingly and its work has not been limited to what it does in the parishes of the diocese. When Frere first became Visitor he summoned a Visitor's Chapter, which had never been done by his predecessors, and saw every sister and novice separately. Then he visited the various departments and houses and suggested improvements which he thought would add to the general comfort or convenience. When the sisterhood undertook the revision of the Constitution and Rules he gave ready help and took much trouble over some of the points under discussion. He gave the sisters valuable aid in improving the ceremonial and music at professions, and also in the arrangements for the keeping of the jubilee in 1933.

After years of waiting he gave permission for the Reservation of the Blessed Sacrament in the little chapel, but not till he was assured that it was the general desire of the sisters.

Frere was much in sympathy with the desire of some nurses to enter a religious community the work of whose members should be sick nursing. He believed in 'a vocation within a vocation', and encouraged the Community of the Epiphany to assist in the formation of the Community of Christ the Consoler, of which all members are state-registered nurses. When he resigned the see of Truro he continued his interest in the new Community and for some years was their Visitor. He helped them to draw up their Rule, and gave them much valuable advice and instruction.

Such were some of the more obvious effects of the Bishop's connexion with the life of religious communities. But they give no idea of the help given to them by his personality and his deep spirituality. 'Those seem to me to inspire and lift one up to heavenly places,' writes a sister, 'and to renew one's sense of the height of the Religious Vocation.'

The diocese has the sole establishment surviving of a kind of which there were until a century ago others at St. Buryan and at St. Crantock, as well as in other places in England. On the north coast, in a district formerly extremely isolated, is the parish of St. Endellion, with its college of prebendaries, the rector, himself a prebendary, at their head. As far as parochial administration is concerned St. Endellion—who is more correctly Endelienta—is on ordinary lines, but it also possesses these immemorial prebends. Their very names are a delight—Bodmin, or King's; Mornays; Trehaverock; besides the rector's St. Endellion. There is a close of small ancient prebendal houses apart from the larger house of the rector. Each prebend has an income, a modest income, and of late years they have all been held by priests whom it is desired to honour or whose income to augment.

In an article in the *Truro Diocesan Gazette* of May 1929, the Bishop wrote that St. Endellion was first mentioned in a document of 1260, and that it suddenly appeared then as a

prebendal institution with a rector and three other prebendaries. He said that it had now become possible to reassemble
and recognize more fully this unique prebendal church, and
the rector and the three other prebendaries were to be joined
together afresh, after having been isolated units for many
years, into something more of fraternal life. There was no
link between them of government or of financial bond, but
they were now to be associated together in the bond of
prayer and mutual help, and to be recognized again in the
diocese as a prebendal body. Some recognition for the prebendaries of St. Endellion had been secured in the cathedral
when the cathedral statutes were drafted by Benson. The
cathedral chapter had now agreed to the promulgation by the
bishop of statutes restoring to the prebendal body its status
at its own request and with the approval of the patron. Moreover, the prebendaries were authorized to use, as a distinction of their office, an almuce of fur lined with crimson. The
new era was inaugurated in St. Endellion church on 2nd May
1929. There was a solemn Eucharist in the church, at which
the prebendal body assembled probably for the first time for
centuries. Later in the day the Bishop gave an address in
which he made vivid and actual the long shadowy history.

But the freshness and animation of approach which
resulted from Dr. Frere's grasp of the meaning, duties and
essentials of the episcopal office, and enabled him to vivify
what, as in the example of St. Endellion, might have remained a name for the shade of reality that had passed away,
was the outstanding characteristic of his whole administration. There were his confirmations. In his addresses, so
simple and so direct, it was felt that he was drawing on the
rich experience of his own spiritual life. There was a radiation
of spiritual power, a solemnizing of thought, and a concentration of the mind on God. Words can hardly express the
power that he had of encouraging the atmosphere of worship.
He arrived in one rather remote parish on a Saturday evening and talked for a little while to the candidates assembled
to meet him in the church. They might not have seen him

before, but after that talk he was not a stranger. Their number was small, but, as has been said, he seemed not to regard number one way or the other. On the Sunday morning at half-past eight he attended Matins and Litany, the candidates being present in the front of the general congregation. When the Litany had been said he took his place at the chancel step and confirmed them one by one. He went to the altar, celebrated the Eucharist, preaching the sermon, and gave the newly-confirmed their first communion. Afterwards he met them and the rest of the faithful at an informal breakfast. Such a bishop and such a confirmation day became a happy memory of fatherliness and friendliness and homeliness. The little badges that he gave—a knight in armour with the motto 'Faithful'—were treasures with a meaning.

It was to be expected that the Bishop, who as a Mirfield Father had been in request for mission preaching, would take the large opportunity which now opened to him to organize and develop mission work in the diocese. His principal agency for this was the diocesan Evangelistic Council. Besides retreats for both clergy and laity there were many activities of an evangelistic nature which the Bishop initiated or encouraged. For some years a small band of diocesan clergy undertook itinerary missions in the summer months in groups of country parishes, going from place to place in a selected area like the friars of old days. They would spend a day or two in each parish, preaching in church or hall or in the open air, receiving simple hospitality in the homes of the villagers. These missions, in their reality, simplicity and novelty, were of value in arousing interest in the message of the Gospel, in bearing witness to the Church's mission, and in giving help and encouragement to the parish priest.

The Bishop also formed a Society of Women Messengers to help, by similar methods, the women and girls of a parish; or to prepare for a parochial mission; or to assist during its continuance. They were thus designed to supplement in parishes the work already undertaken by the Community of the Epiphany. Mrs. Illingworth,[1] who had had long experience in such work in the diocese of Oxford, came to advise in its foundation and first beginnings.

For some years an annual refresher course for clergy was held in three or four different centres in the diocese. Some well-known priest with special qualifications would be invited by the Bishop to come to give lectures on pastoralia or other subjects connected with ministerial work.

Truro had not the advantage of possessing a diocesan house for retreats, conferences and smaller gatherings. The Community of the Epiphany could make such provision for women and girls; and towards the end of the Bishop's time a small house in the extreme north of Cornwall was available. The Bishop put Lis Escop at the disposal of the diocese for constant use for such purposes. Retreats for the clergy, for the Guild of the Forerunner, and for the laity generally, were regularly held there. It was of course frequently used for other gatherings of various kinds.

The Evangelistic Council also took over responsibility for the summer pilgrimage, which was to become an event of diocesan life. Each year some parish connected with the work or name of a Cornish saint was chosen as the place of pilgrimage. All the clergy and choirs were invited, and, though most of those who attended were from the nearer parishes, some came from long distances. As the pilgrimages were in the holiday season the concourse was swollen by summer visitors. Clergy and choirs, servers, thurifers and banner-bearers, vested in a school and went forth with the Bishop and his attendants and the lay folk, singing as they went to where the portable altar had been set up in the open air, perhaps on some spot which legend particularly associated with the saint. So well established did the custom become that a suitable altar with its furniture was obtained to be kept for the

[1] Associated with Frere in the compilation of the well-known manual of intercession, *Sursum Corda*. Her husband was the distinguished philosopher-theologian, J. R. Illingworth, Rector of Longworth, Berks, where she acted as hostess to the annual 'Holy Party' of the *Lux Mundi* group. Affectionately known to her friends as 'Mrs. I.'.

pilgrimages. At this the Eucharist is celebrated. Afterwards
the pilgrims scatter for luncheon and exploration. A lecture
is provided in the afternoon. Sometimes the Bishop gave it;
sometimes the late Dr. Doble, who succeeded Canon Thomas
Taylor of St. Just-in-Penwith as the chief diocesan authority
on Celtic Christianity.

Connected with this interest in the Cornish saints is the
story of the Cornish Kalendar; and here the record enters the
liturgical region which the Bishop had already so widely and
so thoroughly explored from the earliest age of the Church.
In compliance with a resolution of the diocesan synod in 1927
the Bishop appointed a small committee to draw up a
'Cornish Church Kalendar, containing the names of all the
saints honoured in Cornwall, together with a provision of
proper Collects, Epistles and Gospels'. Their report when
presented was accepted by the Bishop, and the result was
published in 1933. It was authorized for use in the diocese
so long as the services contained in it did not displace any
service prescribed by the Prayer Book.

In 1935 the Bishop published a volume of *Collects,
Epistles and Gospels for the Lesser Feasts according to the
Calendar set out in* 1928. In his preface he speaks of the
'very general and very meagre provision for most of them'
made in that Prayer Book. 'The Saints in the Calendar are
people of marked individuality. It is desirable that their
lives and qualifications for their places in the Calendar
should be well known to the people who go to the service
on their days.' A large number of the collects were composed by the Bishop himself; the remainder were drawn
from various sources. This volume was followed, in 1938,
by a supplement, or 'companion', including, for each saint's
day, a brief biographical note, prefixed to the collect and
scriptures, 'intended to help those who are not too well
equipped with knowledge about these heroes of our Christian faith'.

The story of Prayer Book revision as far as it went, and of
Frere's share in it, is told elsewhere in the record. Here it is

necessary only to recall how, as a bishop of the province, he presented the matter to his diocese.

First and foremost he acted through the synod. The synod convened to deal with the matter was the second which he held (the first had been on a disciplinary case). His general attitude had by 1928 become: 'The change from 1927 to 1928 ought not to have been made, but having been made, it ought to be obeyed.' It may be observed that throughout the controversy he showed minor interest in what the State might say or do; that seemed to him comparatively irrelevant to the fundamental consideration of the Church's welfare assured by the Church's authority.

On the 11th Oct. 1928 the synod was held. The Bishop had in the August issue of the *Diocesan Gazette* published an article on the question of where the authority for Reservation lay. Another view was in September presented in an article by a priest of the diocese. The Bishop held that the authority for Reservation was in the bishop, the priest that it belonged to the parish priest *ex officio*. In the November number the Bishop was able to give a summary of the voting on preliminary questions which had been circulated to the clergy and on the resolutions submitted.

Prayer Book revision was also before the Diocesan Conference in January 1928 and in February 1929. On the former occasion the new book—that is, of 1927—was accepted as a legitimate alternative use by the vote of the large majority of the Conference.

The priest just mentioned as stating his counter-view was Nicolo Bernard Walke, who now comes into the story as Vicar of St. Hilary, near Penzance. Round the Vicar of St. Hilary gathered a congregation amazingly constituted for an out-of-the-way Cornish parish. In London it would have been remarkable, not for the ordinary parochial works, but for an appeal which would have gone far beyond the parish. Even at St. Hilary the appeal was irrespective of the parish boundaries. In his book about his Cornish parish Walke declares that he had not learnt to understand the Cornish.

But Walke went straight for the human in people, and it would be more correct to say that he failed to understand them only when suspicious secretiveness put up a barrier.

The church of St. Hilary, the scene of this adventure in religion, is a fine church, but not of special architectural note except that it has a spire—not usual in Cornwall. In Walke's incumbency altar after altar, ornament after ornament, were put into it. Some of the ornaments were extraordinary, but they all meant something in religion or love, and they were brought into an inner unity by that fact and into outer unity by artistic taste. A writer on the church of St. Hilary once suggested that if there had never been a breach between Rome and England to interrupt the interaction of influence it was probable that our English churches would have come to be much like St. Hilary.

It could not but be that such a bishop as Frere would appreciate rightly such a priest as Walke.[1] Indeed, the Bishop always respected work: and here was work, various and some of it unique, by a truly human person whose name was known wherever broadcasting reached. Yet the Bishop himself was unique too, and a compendium of that learning, theological, historical and liturgical, which had so small a portion in Walke; he had an acute sense of corporate obligation, of which likewise Walke's portion was small; he had lived under the discipline of community rule for many years. There is no need to disfigure the story of Frere's episcopate with the wretched details of the Protestant attack, within and without the law, in St. Hilary. The end of the story was not reached in his time. Brawling in the church was a later development. So was the denunciation of Walke, who could

---

[1] Though far from sharing many of Walke's opinions, the Bishop was always ready to mingle humour with his treatment of him—a quality in which both men abounded. He once told how on his first visit to St. Hilary Walke greeted him with the question, 'Would your lordship prefer to be received in the ordinary way or as a Catholic bishop?'; to which he replied, 'I think I should like to be received as a Catholic bishop.' He added that he certainly was! When asked by a friend what Walke's views were on some point, he replied dryly, 'Rather Tridentine, I should think.' [C.S.P.]

do work that nobody else did, by heavy-handed judicial authorities. Let it suffice to put on record that the Bishop strove both to find a settlement which would bring St. Hilary within the bounds of orderliness (a favourite word of his) and at the same time to do his best to protect it from bigoted attack and from automatic legalism.

At this point something may be said about another case which caused some stir in Cornwall. Delabole is a part of the parish of St. Teath, and the huge excavation of its slate quarry, which has roofed churches and houses and provided slabs for north Cornwall for centuries, is known to all travellers to the extremity of the Southern Railway. The district has a church of its own and is worked separately from the mother church. When Frere came to the diocese Delabole church was very much alive. The priest in charge had a large following. He, like Walke, was a man of one piece, though the piece was different, and the gospel preached at Delabole was indistinguishably ecclesiastical and socialist. The priest was of the Thaxted type, and the strength of his social convictions was equalled by the unusual form of their expression. If Walke was in the kindred of St. Francis, the priest of Delabole appeared to be in the succession of John Ball.

The extreme conservatism of Cornwall has been mentioned. Much offence was taken at the opinions reported from Delabole. Wisdom would have left the whole matter alone to flare up and fizzle out, but unfortunately Delabole became 'news', and the local journals gave preposterous advertisement to the sayings and doings there. This would not have been of much consequence, and might even have served as a stimulant for surrounding inertia, but some of the church-people in the diocese lost their heads over the business and took it up with a seriousness which in retrospect is almost unbelievable. They advocated disciplinary action, they wanted to starve out the priest, and the Protestant underworld took the opportunity to divert a little of the odium to the Bishop. The Bishop held an enquiry at Delabole, and those who had set themselves to get rid of the priest pressed

the matter further at a diocesan conference. But the Bishop
was loyal, not only to the priest, but to justice. It is true that
a good deal had been said at Delabole which was unwise, but
nothing which was unorthodox. If the priest had been bene-
ficed no action could have been taken to deprive him, and as
that was so it would have been unjust to take away his
licence in response to clamour. The Bishop stood firm,
though (as the priest admitted) he was the only bishop in
England who would have done so; and showed himself not
unworthy of his great predecessor Henry of Exeter, who had
upheld George Rundle Prynne. And after all this Delabole
cooled down.

It was noteworthy how little these fusses seemed to disturb
the Bishop's otherworldliness. His estimate of the relative
importance of things was not as that of other men. At the
time when one of these difficulties was exciting the diocese
the Bishop was asked if he was not bothered about it. 'Not
nearly as much', he said, 'as I am about ———', naming a
priest who was in much spiritual trouble at the time.

The Diocesan Conference has just been mentioned. His
trust in its judgment was remarkable. He treated it as we
should imagine he treated a chapter at Mirfield when he was
Superior. Suppressing himself he allowed everyone to speak.
There were many good speakers, though some of them
attempted, as the Bishop did not, to impose their will on the
conference. Sometimes a draft carefully prepared by the
standing committee was entirely altered by the conference.
But the Bishop always allowed the members of the conference to give their decision even when, if they had known the
Bishop's mind, they would have arrived at a different result.
There were those who doubted the wisdom of such self-
repression. His veto he was never known to use.

Let us turn to a congenial friendship which resulted in the
production of a book the like whereof no other English
diocese seems to have. Its genesis has been described by the
Bishop himself:

'Ten years ago when the new inhabitants of Lis Escop

were beginning to settle in, there appeared among its earliest visitors a very tall slim figure, of unusually bright colouring and light blue eyes, stooping slightly as if he was ashamed of being so much taller than other people, but beaming with humour and vivacity. Such was Charlie Henderson, for by that name everybody in Cornwall knew him. At once on a very slight provocation he began to pour out a welcome stream of information about Cornwall to the new-comers: not merely historical knowledge, but personal reminiscences humorous and characteristic. I soon found myself sitting at his feet and beginning to learn about the Duchy and its history and its traditions and its characteristics and all the rest. This was not merely a matter of sitting in chairs and listening and questioning; it soon developed into plans of exploration, or rather personally conducted tours, while the stream of information and comment went on continuously. Out of this speedily grew the idea of the *Cornish Church Guide*, and as a result of that more tours and exploration in order that he might fill up some gap in his knowledge and that incidentally the bishop might gain a better acquaintance with his diocese.

'There is so far as I know nothing like it available for any other diocese in the country. The history of churches and parishes was all there; it needed only to be transferred to paper, which was speedily done with skill as much as with accuracy, and the Guide appeared. But it remains a sketch of the bigger project which, alas, remains unfinished, namely the *Complete History of Cornwall and its Parishes*. A lifetime had been given to accumulating the materials; it was a short lifetime, as it proved to Cornwall's great loss; but it was continuous and laborious; the beginnings of his historical research went back to his school-boy days, while his last work was done on the eve of his death. Another remarkable feature of the case was his memory; for side by side with the accumulation of documents and notes, and the result of his searching, there was a very retentive memory which alone made possible the pouring out of a stream of knowledge such as has been described above. . . .'

The Bishop wrote that at the end of 1933. On the 24th September Charles Henderson had died in Rome at the age of thirty-three, 'the greatest historian Cornwall has ever had'.

The Bishop's visitation in the technical sense was undertaken in connexion with the diocesan Jubilee, and characteristically prepared for by his putting into the *Gazette* a retrospect of the theory of diocesan supervision and its exercise by visitation. He explained how the duty of visitation affected the formation of dioceses; how archdeacons and rural deans came to be in the system; and described visitations in the ninth and thirteenth centuries and at the Reformation.

As has been said, the visitation was associated with the Jubilee of the foundation of the diocese in 1878. This was observed from the 22nd April, the second Sunday after Easter, to the following Sunday, and was the greatest diocesan event of the episcopate. Here is part of an account of it (not by the Bishop), written at the time in the *Diocesan Gazette* in the form of 'A Letter to the Future'. Says the imaginary letter-writer:

'The leading idea of our commemoration has been to have an octave in which the diocese might come up to the mother church. The arrangements were made by a committee. I shall not tell you a single name, for it is the work that matters, not the workers. We went on the second Sunday after Easter, the 22nd April, to Sunday, April the 29th. The Evensong of the first Sunday was for the parishes of the city; the Evensong of St. Mark's day was a civic service, attended by mayors and corporations and other public bodies of the diocese; Holy Communion on the Saturday was for the General Chapter; and the evening service that day for the cleric and lay staff of the cathedral. On the other four weekdays the diocese came up in pilgrimage by groups of deaneries: on Monday the 23rd, South Carnmarth, Kerrier and Bodmin; on Tuesday, North Carnmarth, Pydar and West Wivelshire; on Thursday, Trigg Major and Minor, Stratton, East Wivelshire and St. Austell; on Friday, Powder and

Penwith. I confess that not every parish attended. Some did not catch on to the idea; some were hindered by difficulty of transit, for that facility is not in these days what it will be in yours. But anyhow the people came up in numbers which had not been looked for. And to what did these pilgrims come? Each morning at 11.0 the Eucharist was sung; each evening at 6.0 there was a special service at which the Bishop welcomed the pilgrims, and for this service the deaneries were responsible. The form of it, and indeed all the printed matter of the jubilee, you will find collected in the cathedral archives. In the afternoon the pilgrims were taken round the cathedral in parties, and for each group of deaneries a paper had been prepared giving all the special points of connexion between the parishes of that group and the cathedral. These papers are valuable; look them up; they will be of use to you. All the treasures of the Sacristy were on view. The pilgrims were all over the place. Organists went to the organ; ringers to the belfry; naughty boys to giddy heights. The atmosphere of interest and hominess is what you are used to; but I think that I mark a stage in its coming. . . .'

And the reader must try to imagine the Bishop as permeating the whole celebration, throwing himself into it, taking his part in its services, welcoming its congregations, always with the radiant dignity which was his special gift of presence.

In the diocese of Truro the bishop has a good deal of patronage. Some of his appointments which seemed inexplicable were perhaps the consequence of his cool detached view of his duty. What he looked at was a man's work rather than his label, for, in spite of his own decided Churchmanship on a definite line and his constant contact with the parties in the Church, his realization of these differences was a matter of knowledge rather than of feeling; and it is feeling that embitters. His general attitude is illustrated by what happened in the vacancy of a benefice near Truro. He offered it to the incumbent of another parish, who might be described as an Anglo-Catholic, with the remark that the congregation was old fashioned, 'but you would not mind that as much as some'. When it was refused he made the offer to an incumbent who was prominently Evangelical. The reader will see the two points. In the first offer it was assumed that the priest would suit himself to the congregation, and there was no suggestion that he should go to the parish bent on innovation. And when it was refused the Bishop did not confine himself to the same school for further choice, but looked round to see who was doing good work and should have the opportunity of change. Label did not seem to him to matter.[1]

With regard to private patrons he abstained from trying to influence them. They had their place and responsibility in the scheme of things and he had his. Each must keep to his own. It was to that effect that he had replied on an occasion when a remonstrance was made to him privately about a nomination by a lay patron which seemed nepotistic. He again showed that respect for the responsibilities of other people which has been mentioned as coming out in his chairmanship of the Diocesan Conference.

Much the same might be said of the appointment to honorary canonries. No bishop ever packed a chapter less. His reasons for appointments were sometimes obscure and remote from the considerations that seem ordinarily to govern these matters. A friend hinted at surprise on one occasion. 'Well,' said the Bishop, 'I went into the man's study and saw his books and that he was a reading man.'

[1] His attitude finds clear expression in a letter written in 1929 to Sir Michael Sadler:
My whole heart and soul is on the side of comprehension. I believe that what the English Church can contribute to the world is the conviction that Churchmen can live together, resting on a deep basis of the fundamentals of the Faith, whilst at the same time differing markedly as to superstructure. When I say 'faith' I perhaps also ought to say 'faith and discipline', because I think it is becoming more and more clear that not only is a fundamental agreement in faith required, if there is to be a real unity, but that, for different reasons and of quite a less important character, there must be agreement of system and discipline. My hope is that we can go on patiently getting to understand others and helping them to understand one another; hastening slowly because of divisions in the Church of England which, although they distress me, are diversities rather than divisions.

Indeed, Frere seemed sometimes to be curiously tangential in his opinion of people.

So also he treated the *Diocesan Gazette*. The *Gazette* was the successor of the *Church in the West*, which was the organ of the Exeter diocese before the division and, for some time after, of the two dioceses. It had had varying fortune, and at the Diocesan Conference of 1927 was reconstituted by an arrangement on which it must make its own way in independence or perish. It had its critics, one of them, very occasionally, in private, the Bishop. He always, however, respected the original arrangement, and made no attempt to diminish the independence. Probably in no other diocese would the bishop have shown this restraint.

'Bodrean', the name of a country house in the parish of St. Clement, calls to mind an enterprise which carried on bravely from 1933 until its work was ended by the conditions of the war. For a year the project had been before the diocese, prayed for by intercession groups, and the subject of a campaign by Brother Douglas of the Franciscan Friars of Cerne Abbas. The house was bought and the home established and maintained as a place of hope for wayfaring men—those who tramp the roads (and having reached Cornwall must needs turn back again) and have nowhere to go but the casual ward and the common lodging-house. 'Bodrean' was not meant to be a lodging-house with amenities, but to provide such rest and training and employment as each individual case required, a place where lives could be repaired and given a fresh start. Such work was dear to the Bishop's heart, and showed the diocese an aspect of him which without it might have remained unappreciated. When he came to bless 'Bodrean' on the occasion of its opening by the Lord-Lieutenant he related the trouble with which they were dealing to our Lord's story of the labourers in the market-place, and pointed out that unemployment was one of the standing problems of the world.

There is little doubt that he made demands upon his physical strength beyond what prudence would have advised.

Not only were his days full, but when diocesan business was over and Compline said with the brethren and staff, he would, more often than not, sit up till a late hour of the night, engaged in historical or liturgical research, and yet would be in his place without fail in the chapel at seven o'clock next morning for Matins and Eucharist. Apart from a month's holiday in September and the August house-party at Lis Escop described elsewhere, the Bishop allowed himself very little recreation. Indeed he seemed constitutionally unable to relax the bow. Even his constant journeys by road were made opportunities for study; and he devised an ingenious arrangement for a small electric light to fall on his book.

We reach a culminating scene in this story. For eight years the Bishop had ruled the diocese. There had been some misunderstanding, some prejudice, much misrepresentation. He had moved calmly through each difficulty, wearing it away by the sheer force of grace and goodness, every year winning more and more of those who could admire the scholar and the still greater number of those who learnt to love and revere the saint. It was determined that there should be a memorial of such an episcopate, and that future generations should see in a portrait what manner of man was this new manner of bishop. A committee, with the then Rector of Blisland as its secretary, had no difficulty in raising the funds for a portrait. The commission to paint it was given to Mr. Harold Knight, who represented the Bishop 'as a simple Father of the Community of the Resurrection, rather than in the ceremonial vestments of a prince and prelate of the Church'. The portrait is an heirloom at Lis Escop. A replica is at Mirfield.[1]

A great crowd assembled at Lis Escop for the presentation on the 28th September 1933. Fine weather enabled it to be in the open air. The occasion was indeed moving and memor-

[1] A reproduction of this portrait forms the frontispiece of the volume issued by the Alcuin Club after Frere's death with the title *Walter Howard Frere: A collection of his papers on liturgical and historical subjects* (Oxford Univ. Press 1940).

able. It was the high point of the episcopate. The Bishop had
come into his own in the heart of the diocese. The words of
the Archdeacon of Cornwall were a summary of the matter:

'Our business this afternoon is one which is very gratify-
ing to ourselves; and, we hope, not unwelcome to your
Lordship. It is the outcome of a long cherished desire to be
able to give some outward and vocal expression to our feelings of loyalty and devotion to yourself; a sentiment very
deeply felt, and very widely held. Such feeling has, no doubt,
for the most part, to remain latent and silent; but it has been
eagerly anxious to find an opportunity of public expression.
Coupled with this desire is the wish to be able to secure some
visible and permanent record of your Lordship's outward
form and semblance, for future generations.

'The portrait which, in a few moments, we shall ask you
to accept, comes as a gift from both clergy and laity, from
men and women of all kinds and classes; within your diocese
and from beyond it. It is the offering of very full hearts:
hearts full of respect, gratitude and affection.

'We feel respect for your person and your office; for your
great gifts of scholarship and wide learning; for your powers
of wise administration; above all, for the example of your
life and character; which indeed, I sometimes feel, by reason
of its simplicity, its humanity, its unworldliness, its geniality,
may tend to conceal from the undiscerning the greatness of
the man. We feel gratitude for your eminent services, both
to the Church at large, and to this diocese in particular; for
your ungrudging and unremitting labours, day in and day
out, for our spiritual welfare; for your individual kindness
and generosity; and for your faithful diligence as the pastor
of your flock.

'We have feelings not only of respect and gratitude; I
venture to use a more intimate word: we regard you with
feelings of personal affection. We look upon you not only as
our ecclesiastical superior, to whom we are happy to render
loyal obedience; not only as a leader whose guidance we
trustfully follow; not only as a teacher with a unique gift of

making profound truths intelligible to the simple-minded; but as our personal Friend and Father in God.'

With that in mind pass to the closing scene eighteen months later. At the beginning of 1935 the Bishop came to the decision that failing health made it his duty to resign the see. As long before as 1930 he had been ill through over-work, and the *Diocesan Gazette* of June that year contained an appeal (published without his knowledge) to the diocese to spare him as much as might be. For nearly five years longer he bore the burden, and then quietly and definitely resigned. The see became vacant at midnight on Friday, the 15th February. On the two Sundays preceding, the last of the Bishop's pastoral letters had been read in the churches. It had not (*more suo*) said a word about the resignation. It was a missions pastoral, urging the duty of missionary work 'because mankind is all one family'.

He had not spoken of himself in the pastoral letter. But in the Bishop's brief notes in the February *Gazette* there was this:

The Last Note.

'The last note is of
farewell, not so much sad in
my ears, as thankful to God:
and grateful to Cornwall. But
it has stolen half my heart.'

W. T.

6

HOLIDAY INTERMEZZO:
AUGUST AT LIS ESCOP

by C. S. Phillips

O nce in the loggia at Lis Escop the Bishop's sister, Mrs. Wilfred Barnes, said to the present writer half-jokingly, 'When Walter's life comes to be written, there must be a chapter on the Truro Augusts, and you and I must do it together.' But, as things turned out, she was to die before her brother, and if the chapter is to be written, the survivor must attempt the grateful task alone.

What follows claims to be no more than a kind of 'holiday snapshot', a casual and sometimes rather frivolous record of happy days. But such things may sometimes be more revealing than a formal studio portrait; and it seems right too that a book so concerned with deep and serious matters as this should say something about its subject on his lighter side, especially as the absurd notion of the 'monk-bishop' as a consistently remote and rather forbidding person was never completely banished from the popular mind. Indeed, one even remembers a man of some distinction (who really should have known better) speaking of him as though he were a kind of embodiment of ecclesiastical rigour and obscurantism!

The 'Truro Augusts' began in the first summer of Frere's episcopate (1924). They were never entirely a 'holiday' for the Bishop himself; his own holiday in the (or rather *his*) complete sense being taken in September, usually in the form of a brief and very strenuous motor-tour on the Continent. But the diocese gave him less to do in August than at most other seasons, and he was thus at liberty to devote a good deal of time to his family and friends, and to provide them with the sort of holiday which, set against the romantic background of Cornwall, will always glow with a kind of enchantment in the memory of those who shared in it. For five weeks or so the two Fathers who lived with the Bishop were on holiday themselves; the normal routine of a 'cell' of Mirfield was temporarily suspended (apart from a celebration in the chapel every morning, to which guests might or might not go as they pleased); and Lis Escop became for the time being a pleasant if rather sketchily furnished country house—though, to be sure, when a newly-arrived guest once innocently spoke of the hall as 'the lounge', he was courteously but promptly corrected.

As a 'holiday home' the house could hardly have been better. Its situation on the hill-side lifted it well above the city of Truro, which is apt to be distinctly stuffy in summer; and its garden was a beautiful place, though Frere himself had none of the gardening enthusiasm of his predecessor, Bishop C. W. Stubbs, and of his successor, Bishop Hunkin, who have done so much to make it what it is. From one corner of the terrace there is an exquisite view of the cathedral, and on Sundays and practice-nights the sonorous tones of its magnificent old bells could be heard rising from below. Indoors, bedrooms were abundant—monkishly austere with their usual furniture of an iron bedstead with scarlet top-blanket, a chest of drawers and a chair, with a gas-ring in the hearth to boil one's hot water. Downstairs, the big double drawing-room was very undrawing-room-like and scarcely furnished at all; but across the hall was the noble dining-room—another legacy of Bishop Stubbs and furnished for Frere in a simple but dignified fashion by his friends—to supply an element of episcopal state. Of this one was always glad; for in spite of a propensity for shabby clothes and (on occasion) for squalid surroundings,[1] the Bishop was essentially *grand seigneur*. Outwardly and inwardly, there was something about him that called to mind Fénelon at Cambrai; and this innate breeding and distinction made him a figure for which the stately proportions and splendid old tapestries of the Lis Escop dining-room appeared the proper background. Some such gracious environment, too, seemed to befit one who so well embodied that combination of learning, culture and a refined, unostentatious spirituality which represents the Anglican ethos at its best. With him one felt in authentic contact with the tradition that finds expression equally in Bishop Andrewes in the seventeenth century and in Dean Church in the nineteenth.

During the 'Truro Augusts' the nucleus of the party was always more or less the same. There were first of all the Bishop's sister Lucy and her husband, Wilfred Barnes, accompanied in the earlier years by their schoolboy sons, David and Michael. The Bishop's niece Audrey (Arthur Frere's daughter) was sometimes there as well. Then there were a few privileged friends who were expected every year, including Miss Ethelwyn Pearson, a friend of the Bishop and his sisters from early days, and (towards the end) Dr. H. C. Colles, *The Times* music critic, and his wife. Those who came less regularly, but a number of times, included Mrs. Stuart Moore (Evelyn Underhill) and her husband, Miss Eleanor and Miss Christiana Gregory, close friends since the early days of their father's reign as Dean of St. Paul's, and Dr. Henry Ley of Eton and Mrs. Ley. In addition there would be a stream of visitors for a night or two—bishops and dignitaries on holiday or on missionary deputation, parsons from the

---

[1] One remembers a funny account by one of the Community of a long tramp round Strasbourg at the end of a day's journey, as he and Frere, carrying heavy bags, searched for a hotel sufficiently deplorable to satisfy the latter. At last his companion exclaimed, 'Walter, I can't go another step until I have something to eat and drink.' 'All right,' replied Frere, 'let's go in here'—and led the way down some basement steps into a small sordid-looking *estaminet* of the 'Good pull up for carmen' type.

diocese and Fathers from Mirfield,[1] scholar- and musician-friends—musicians were always sure of a special welcome. Twice at least a charming French abbé was there, who delighted to attend *la messe de Monseigneur* and one day rather startled some fellow-guests in Truro by informing them that 'our lord has gone into the cathedral'. . . . A most miscellaneous company—the Old Guard used to call it the 'Truro Pie'; but the ingredients seemed to mingle well, and the continued coming and going was always exciting.

How pleasant it was for the traveller by that prince among trains, the Cornish Riviera express, to emerge from Truro station just before four o'clock and see the sturdy uniformed figure and beaming face of Weeks the chauffeur, waiting by the Bishop's car to take him up to Lis Escop! There the Bishop (unless he happened to be absent from home) would come out of his study to greet his guest and to insist on carrying his bag upstairs. Protests were in vain, and the baffled guest usually followed his host in a rather rebellious frame of mind; though memory records no incident quite so piquant as Dr. Prestige's picture of the aged Bishops Talbot and Gore wrestling at the top of a London staircase and Gore shouting, 'You silly old ass, you shall *not* carry it down'. Then downstairs to meet the rest of the company at tea, unless a long day's expedition was in progress.

The ménage, as will have been gathered, was very simple—even quaintly so for those accustomed to the ministrations of butlers and parlourmaids. Once when a dignified couple were spending a week-end at Lis Escop for some official engagement, a fellow-guest who happened to be round the corner of a corridor overheard the wife remark, 'What an extraordinary establishment!' But the admirable Mrs. Stephens and her helpers kept the house clean and tidy, and food was simple, but abundant and excellent. It is not true

[1] One who specially lingers in the memory is the late Fr. G. W. Hart—in his last years a martyr to arthritis, yet none the less always full of gaiety and laughter and absolutely refusing to be daunted from scrambling up hills or over rocks with the rest. It was a miracle how he managed to do it.

that the Bishop cleaned his guests' boots (as has been reported); but there is good reason for believing that he was not above cleaning his own—one always hopes that the story is true which makes Weeks tell a fellow-chauffeur that it was 'because no one else is fit to do it'. At meals the Bishop himself took the lead in serving his guests, in the removal of dirty plates and in stacking them on a trolley for transfer to the kitchen, and in clearing the tables when the meal was over. (He was very handy with a crumb-brush.) To be allowed to help him was a privilege in which no woman might share, strictly reserved for members of his family or of the Community and a few of the oldest habitués. The eager offers of others to help were politely refused. For many of his guests all this was rather embarrassing; and it is more than unlikely that the diocesan laity in particular ever really enjoyed being waited on by their Bishop. But it was part of the monastic idea; and the Bishop would allow no departure from it. Certainly he always did his share of it as though it were the most natural thing imaginable; and it was the same when he rendered similar services in a rectory or vicarage where there were no servants.

For the first hours after breakfast the guests were left to their own devices, for the Bishop had his correspondence to attend to. This he managed with the aid of a dictaphone, of which the cylinders were duly removed by his devoted secretary, Mr. Swete, and transcribed later in the day. The time taken by the Bishop over his letters depended, of course, on their number and importance. Sometimes we had reason to believe that the burden of them was being increased by the controversies and 'rows' which from time to time disturbed his episcopate. But he himself never talked diocesan 'shop'; and he was the last person to encourage such talk in others, though one or two of us might be allowed a glimpse of the more grotesque of the anonymous postcards that were liable to arrive when the Cornish love of controversy waxed warm, and were speedily consigned to the waste-paper basket. The Bishop bore the attacks of his critics with calm dignity and, as far as possible, in silence; his only comment being to say now and then to his house-mates of the Community, 'If only it weren't *Christians* who were doing it!' But it would be a great mistake to suppose that he didn't *feel* them, or the incidents from which they arose. Once, at a time when one of the usual diocesan volcanoes was erupting, a friend commented on the piles of abstruse books and papers on liturgical or similar subjects that lay on a table in his study. 'Oh,' said the Bishop, 'it isn't that table that worries me, it's the other'—pointing to the table on which the diocesan correspondence was ranged.[1]

For the most part, however, the Bishop had finished his letters by noon, and often well before, and was then ready to start on one of the expeditions which took place nearly every day and were often skilfully fitted in with various episcopal duties—institutions, calls on the clergy, etc. The arrangements for these expeditions were left entirely to him, for experience proved that, if they were not, confusion was sure to result. As they were always made by car, the number taking part would depend on the number of cars available; but what with the Bishop's own car, the Barnes's little two-seater 'Evangeline' (in the dickey of which the Bishop himself would often insist on riding, looking as though he were sitting on a pontifical throne), and such cars as members of the house-party had brought with them, it was seldom that anyone who wanted to go had to be left behind.

The majority of the party being no longer very young, and inclined to be serious in their tastes—anxious, too, to see as much of Cornwall as possible—the expeditions would usually take the form of visits to the places of interest in

---

[1] The following anecdote may be worth recording. On one occasion the Bishop was instituting a new incumbent. He was the first presentee of a party trust of pronounced hue which had recently acquired the patronage; and, as the traditions of the parish were of a different colour, there were some misgivings as to what would happen. Before the service the incumbent said in a rich brogue, 'Hwhat hymns would you like, my Lord?' The Bishop replied, 'What do you suggest?' 'How about "Fight the good fight"?' 'I think "Peace, perfect peace" would be much better.'

which the Duchy is so rich; though if any younger folk preferred sea-bathing to scenery or antiquities, every facility was
given them for indulging their taste and rejoining the others
later. The Bishop's own zest for sight-seeing, as for so many
other things, was immense and tireless. As he once said in a
rare moment of self-revelation, 'I have always wanted to sing
in the chorus and be in the audience as well.' He himself
would usually head the procession in his own car, sitting in
front next to Weeks, sometimes with a map spread out on
his knees to help him to find the way. For him the shortest
route was always the best: he was completely indifferent to
the *quality* of roads. Indeed, 'one of Walter's roads' was a
family expression for a road of exceptional vileness.

Sometimes we would 'do' a round of churches. The
Bishop's imagination, like that of his predecessor Archbishop Benson, was fired by the romantic traditions of early
Cornish Christianity; and he loved to shew his visitors the
monuments that it and later ages have left behind. He was
particularly interested in the square carved bench-ends which
are a feature of the churches of the west; and at one period
his guests might be seen now and then dotted about a church,
sitting on the floor on hassocks to list or sketch them. Later
on Wilfred Barnes, a real artist with the camera, made a fine
collection of photographs of them which the Bishop presented to the County Museum at Truro.[1]

The Bishop, however, was interested not only in the relics
of Christian Cornwall; he was also keen to explore those of
its pagan predecessor. Thus the day's objective would sometimes be 'prehistorics'. These he would be indefatigable in
tracking down and examining, forcing his way through the
narrowest and darkest *foggous* or into the most uninviting-
looking 'beehive-huts', often so like broken-down pigsties.
Many of them were in remote spots very difficult to find; but

[1] His original idea was to embody them in a monograph, with letterpress
by himself. But no publisher appeared to be willing to sponsor the project,
and the Bishop's conscience forbade him to spend on it money that might be
useful in other ways. For Frere authorship was seldom a paying occupation.

the Bishop would lead the way across the moors for those
who cared to follow him, his tall slim figure moving up hill
and down dale with that astonishingly light, almost dancing,
step of his. He seemed well nigh to float up the steepest
inclines, so that those toiling behind him felt that they would
hardly be surprised if he suddenly indulged in the saintly
practice of 'levitation'. Sometimes, again, we would visit the
beauty-spots of the wonderful Cornish coast. But it is hard
to say how far the Bishop himself was interested in scenery
for its own sake. Certainly he enjoyed natural beauty, but he
was not disposed to linger in admiring it. One often wished,
when his health began to fail, that he could be content just to
lie back in some quiet spot and drink in the loveliness of sky
and sea. But that was not his way—perhaps he might even
have regarded it as a waste of time. His religion, one sus-
pects, was always concentrated on the unseen rather than on
the seen. In the same way, he had a deep distrust of the
merely 'æsthetic' side of religion.[1]

Lunch was usually taken *al fresco* out of baskets—Cornish
pasties or sandwiches to eat, Cornish cider to drink. The
Bishop opened the baskets and dispensed the viands, but
himself hardly ate anything. Then on for more sight-seeing
till it was time for tea—out of baskets and thermos-flasks
again, or sometimes at a 'Teas Provided' place—the latter
usually meant Cornish cream. The programme more often
than not was terribly overloaded; with the result that the
return journey had to be made *allegro molto feroce* across Bodmin Moor or through Camborne and Redruth, if we were
to be home in time for supper.

Supper over, there would be talk for a while—and then
there began for the Bishop, especially if the guests were few
and suitable, what was perhaps the happiest time of all. Now
was the hour for *music*. In the early days, when wireless was
in its babyhood and the Bishop had not yet discovered the

---

[1] Once, when his party eagerly seized an opportunity of seeing the splendid vestments, etc., belonging to a certain church, he himself quietly withdrew,
saying, 'I think I will go and smoke a pipe in the garden.'

WALTER HOWARD FRERE

charms of the gramophone, this had to be mainly home-made. His sister, indeed, had decided that her singing days were over; and her husband, though (or perhaps because) a professional musician, was firm in his refusal to perform. But there might be others who were less modest; and the Bishop himself was never unwilling (though usually only if he were asked) to sing songs in various languages, including Russian.[1] He was no less ready (though something less than a first-rate pianist) to take a hand in pianoforte duets, of which he had quite a good collection—mostly arrangements of classical symphonic and chamber works. (The Brandenburg Concertos, in particular, were a staple article of fare.) Or he would exclaim, 'And now let us have some Wag,' and the *Ring* would be attacked in a rather complicated arrangement for piano duet and the voice parts. For this occasion Wilfred Barnes would make an exception, and he and his wife would be 'primo' and 'secondo'; while others would sing the vocal parts as they could, the Bishop essaying most of the tenor roles and never quailing even before Siegfried's highest notes. . . . All very good fun for the performers, less so for the audience: but on such occasions this had to be small and indulgent. In any case (as is remarked elsewhere) Frere was one of those music-lovers who are much more interested in the music than in the performance: and (as he used to say): 'In music we were brought up to do the best we could, and not to worry too much about the result.' At the same time it cannot be denied that this indifference was a source of perplexity to some. For instance, his old friend, the late Miss Eleanor Gregory, has written, 'What always surprised me, both when playing for him at the Deanery and, later, with his "sing-song" friends at Truro, was that, with all his scholar's passion for accuracy and perfection, he should be

[1] In this Truro period his voice was worn and tired (as is the way of tenors in their sixties). But his singing had not lost the feeling and artistic imagination of his younger days, when (as Fr. Talbot recorded after his death) a visitor to Bishop's House, Kennington, on the afternoon of an ordination asked, 'Who is that man with the face of St. Bruno singing passionate Breton love-songs?'

112

content never to "work up" anything, so as to perform it better. I remember Filson Young once asking me whether in listening to music I heard the actual performance or the "ideal" rendering; and I suppose that it was always from the latter angle that Walter heard music, or at all events the music in which he could join.'

The only kind of 'mechanical music' available at Lis Escop in the early days was a pianola, which had been given to the Bishop by some of his friends. For working this the youthful energies of the 'pontifical nephews' were often called into play; or the Bishop himself would sit down to manipulate the 'roly-poly', as he called it. As long as life lasts some of us will never be able to listen to certain pieces of music— notably the Rachmaninov C minor piano concerto and César Franck's *Variations Symphoniques*—without a picture rising in the mind of the dining-room at Lis Escop on a summer evening, with the Bishop's slim gaitered legs pedalling away, his figure silhouetted in the fading light against the tall french windows behind.

Perhaps this may be a good place to say something about the Bishop's musical preferences. These were unashamedly 'high-brow'—for light music he cared little and things like jazz had simply no existence for him at all. Also the preferences were remarkably constant. The major stars of the musical firmament, of course, never change (except by way of addition), but their relative positions vary somewhat from generation to generation. Frere's tastes were exactly what one might have expected from the *milieu* in which they were formed—the Cambridge of Stanford.[1] In those days Handel, Haydn and Mozart did not enjoy their present cult, at least among the musical intelligentzia; and Frere never cared greatly for any of them. Mozart, possibly, he thought rather frivolous (he was far from having an 'eighteenth-century mind'), just as Chopin seemed to him meretricious—one remembers a scathing comment, 'A typical bit of Chopin

[1] A reference to Dr. Stewart's account on p. 26 will shew how little they changed.

vulgarity'. (Most musicians have their blind spots.) Nor did he care greatly for Beethoven. The supreme gods were Bach, Brahms and Wagner. This last taste may seem rather surprising in one who in other ways so loathed the self-assertive and the grandiose; but here especially his 'period' must be taken into account. For Schumann he had the warm affection characteristic of his generation; and Schubert (especially the songs), Dvořák, César Franck, Hugo Wolf and Richard Strauss he loved. He was also much attracted to French folksongs; and one tremendous *buffo* affair from Burgundy, with a chorus beginning '*Oh! la perdriole*', was wont to become a perfect riot as he sang it. The great Russians were familiar to him at a time when England had hardly heard of them; and he developed (rather late) a strong liking for the best of Elgar. Nor did he fail to do his best to keep in touch with later developments: he was always anxious not to be *arriéré* in music or in anything else. The latest of all rather baffled his earnest efforts after comprehension—Béla Bartók for example. But the French impressionists he greatly enjoyed: he loved the Duparc and Fauré songs, and a broadcast performance of *Pelléas et Mélisande* once gave him some four hours of rapt delight. He subscribed to the Sibelius Society, and he was a good deal interested in Stravinsky, though more in the earlier than in the later works. Among recent English composers he greatly admired both Vaughan Williams and Delius.

In the last years at Truro the element of home musicmaking rather fell into the background, apart from the Tuesday evening sing-songs described elsewhere; possibly because we were none of us quite so young as formerly, possibly too because the company may have tended, on the whole, to become more heterogeneous. The pianola was now usually silent; but the gramophone and the wireless had asserted their sway. The Bishop's radio-gramophone was kept in the hall; and this had the advantage of allowing him to steal a little music for himself in the evening without boring those of his guests who did not care for it. He had not a great deal of small-talk, and in those years was often ailing and very tired. So after supper he would quietly leave the general company in the dining-room to play bridge or make conversation, and slip away to have a spell of music with anyone who cared to join him, usually to the accompaniment of a pipe. (He was very fond of his pipe, and of a good cigar now and then when anybody gave him one: cigarettes he despised). Unfortunately the 'set' was not a very good one; and his hatred of spending money on himself forbade him to get anything new and better. Nor had he any particular talent for mechanics. Thus not infrequently he would patiently sit and twiddle the knobs, but nothing happened. Once he had been looking forward greatly to a broadcast performance of *Tristan* from Bayreuth. But alas! nothing came through save an occasional faint murmur. Dr. Colles said afterwards that, as he sat with his head pressed close up against the set, he looked like a starving man gazing through bars at the food that was beyond his reach.

Fortunately it was by no means always so; and some of the Bishop's most blissful hours were spent in 'listening-in'. His enthusiasm for listening to music was of the kind usually found perhaps in the amateur rather than in the professional, who seems for the most part to avoid a 'busman's holiday'. To join him in doing so was to be given the feeling—more than with anybody one has ever known—that one was sharing in a religious rite. The idea of using music as a 'background' for other things was abhorrent to him. Once at Truro tea arrived as an interesting piece of music was issuing from the loudspeaker. The Bishop at once turned the set off. To an old friend who protested he said, 'You can't eat your tea and listen to music at the same time.'

Enough has been said about Frere's devotion to music—probably a good deal more than enough for the non-musical reader. But unless it is stressed a complete picture of him is impossible. Music, indeed, was the one direction in which he found it easy to 'let himself go'. Temperamentally he was the very opposite of the expansive type: it was not easy for him to open up even to those who knew him well. When a friend confessed to a propensity for getting into conversation with his fellow-travellers in a train, he said, 'Then I shall take good care not to get into the same carriage with you.' With this reserve there went no trace of *gaucherie*. The surface that he presented to the world was astonishingly smooth and brilliant. But it was not an easy matter for any but his close friends to get through to the other side of it; and even they were sometimes puzzled by what in certain ways was a rather enigmatic personality. It was this reserve, coupled with a fear of being insincere, that made him shrink unduly from those quite innocent ways of courting popular goodwill that are almost part of a clergyman's stock-in-trade. (He was much more likely to do something that he knew would make him *un*popular!) This applied to high as to low. Some, for instance, who loved and admired him felt it a pity that he did not make more contact with the Cornish county families, who felt instinctively that he was one of themselves (perhaps that was one reason why they resented his 'socialism' so much), and were always ready to succumb to his charm and accomplishments whenever he gave them the chance. Probably it would have been different if he had been made a bishop not at sixty but at fifty, when the marvellous adaptability that he shewed in his great Mirfield period was still unimpaired. Yet it cannot be denied that throughout his life there were those who found him really formidable, and declared that they could never bring themselves to open their hearts to him—a fact which no one would have regretted more than himself.

Perhaps all this may be counted a serious drawback in a bishop in a democratic age. But the man was what he was, and he would not pretend to be anything else. One felt that in this and other matters he would have subscribed to Bishop Creighton's favourite doctrine of *Entsagung*—that 'freedom and content are to be obtained only by the recognition of one's own limitations and by self-identification with them, so that what appears as an iron barrier set before one by a remorseless destiny . . . becomes a help rather than a hindrance, for it makes life more definite and its problems more soluble.'[1] (Was this also the explanation of his indifference in his later years to poetry and *belles lettres* generally, as distracting him from his chosen lines of study? All his life the wide range of his interests must have made a real problem for him.) Yet his temperamental lack of 'heartiness' did not mean that he failed to value a greater expansiveness in others, so long, of course, as it was sincere (and, perhaps one should add, not too much brought to bear upon him personally). To quote Miss Gregory again: 'He greatly longed to be able to make contact with people; and I have heard him speak with admiring envy (if I may use the word) of people to whom this came easily. I feel that he was always battling with pride and intense reserve. He little measured his capacity for arousing deep affection and devotion.' He had, for instance, a real admiration for Dick Sheppard (though two good men could hardly have been more unlike), and once said of him that he had 'given a twist to the Church of England that would be permanent'. Nor by any means did he lack the power, when he felt that the occasion warranted it, to indulge in the lighter kinds of talk. No one's conversation (mercifully) savoured less of 'anecdotage' than his. Yet hidden away among the contents of that capacious brain was a fund of good stories, as he proved one evening when the Dean of St. John's Cathedral, New York, was spending the night at Lis Escop, and his host was able to hold his own even in the presence of an accomplished American raconteur.

It may be added that the Bishop conceived a great liking and admiration for the Cornish character, though in many ways it is so unlike his own very English one. To take two examples at random, one remembers his comment, 'What beautiful manners the Cornish people have!', when a labourer went out of his way to open a gate for his car to the accompaniment of a courteous smile, and his delight at the facility of speech shewn by a gathering of largely working-class lay-

[1] *Life and Letters,* i, 106.

men at Lis Escop, 'so different from a lot of tongue-tied Englishmen'.

As regards his religion, this was never in any way obtruded upon his visitors, though they could not but be conscious that it was always at the back of everything else—'You embody for me a way of life and a fabric of belief', wrote Sir Michael Sadler to him during these Truro years. On Sundays his guests were free to go to church or to stay at home as they preferred, and if the younger folk asked whether they could play tennis on the lawn on Sunday afternoon the Bishop readily consented, though it is possible that Cornish Nonconformity was rather shocked. He himself doubtless said his offices privately every day; but during the 'Truro Augusts' only Compline was ever said in the chapel, and then only when it was asked for. (One can still hear the curious high intonation with which he always began the Confession.) At the daily celebration in the chapel he was always present; and when he did not celebrate himself he would serve—kneeling in his stall and going forwards and back as required. He himself always used the 1928 rite; though others might do as they pleased. The service went on its way quickly and very quietly, yet with the perfect clarity and beautiful modulation of voice that always marked the Bishop's utterance. There were no long pauses for private devotions, still less for interpolations from other rites—the Bishop's rule was that 'if you had a rite you should stick to it'. Here, as always in him, one saw a consummate union of dignity with simplicity—he had the art of making ceremonial seem the most natural thing in the world. For example, his handling of a mitre when he had to wear one was incomparable—a perfect exemplar of the advice that he once gave to a fellow-bishop: 'There are really only two rules: Don't pray in it and don't fuss with it.'

On Sundays the Bishop would always celebrate himself in the chapel; and then after breakfast would often go away to preach or confirm; but he managed as a rule to be back in time to preach in the evening in the cathedral, whither his guests would usually walk down to hear him. Truro Cathedral is notoriously a difficult place to speak in; but his clear voice and exquisite articulation made him easily audible wherever one sat. He never raised his voice or worked himself up —perhaps his Celtic hearers would have preferred it if he had, for their race has always provided rare connoisseurs of 'pulpit oratory'. But his way was to reason and persuade, not to perplex, to startle or to storm. All was cool, calm and (like his books) transparently clear. There was plenty of fresh and original thought; but couched in very simple language. Deceptively simple—for the unlearned might be led to think that there was 'nothing much in it', like the old Yorkshire woman who was once overheard by him to say, as the congregation dispersed in the darkness after a sermon of his, 'Nay, a think nowt o' Frere.' The Bishop's simplicity had sometimes the paradoxical result that it was his most intelligent hearers who were the most impressed by his sermon.

Frere's resignation in 1935 put a stop to the 'Truro Augusts', which for the last year or two had been overshadowed by the declining health of his sister and himself. For two years, however, it was possible for him to recapture a little of the old atmosphere in the form of a tour in a borrowed car with Wilfred Barnes and the present writer. In September 1935 the centre was Chiddingfold near Haslemere, whence every day long excursions were made over most of Surrey, and into Sussex, Kent, Hampshire and Wiltshire; and the following September the cream of Yorkshire was visited from Mirfield. His zest for sight-seeing was entirely unabated, as were his gaiety of spirit and caustic wit. One remembers, in a certain southern cathedral, his commenting mischievously on the not very interesting music in the service-list for the week and saying, 'That is the sort of thing that some of you are ready to die in the last ditch for'; then, when it was pleaded that it was only a holiday-time list, he retorted, 'Well, I renounce them all.'

Slowly but steadily his health declined during these last

years; but the spirit rose triumphant over the resistance and failure of the body. Here the self-discipline of a lifetime stood him in magnificent stead. Yet this was not incompatible with a certain relaxing of the bow. The beard which he grew after he left Truro was a kind of symbol of this. When asked why he had grown it, he replied, 'I have shaved every day of my life for over fifty years, and I feel I have earned a rest.' Ascetic he was in many (or most) ways; but from the excesses of asceticism he was saved by two qualities which were his in an eminent degree—a sense of proportion and a sense of humour.

[*The present book purports to be nothing more than a memoir, designed to furnish a portrait of the man Walter Frere as he was and a brief account of the main stages of his career. It is therefore not strictly part of its plan to provide an estimate of his work as a scholar and writer—that is the critic's business, not the biographer's. But Frere was so much a savant by gifts and temperament, and his achievement in this capacity so many-sided, important and influential, that a picture of him and of his life-work could hardly be complete that did not say at least something of his labours in those fields of scholarship which he made his own. For this purpose it is obviously necessary to call in the help of experts, for they alone are competent to pronounce an opinion on subjects at once so various and so recondite as those with which Frere concerned himself. We are therefore much indebted to the distinguished authorities who have contributed three chapters, dealing respectively with Frere as 'The Liturgist', 'The Historian' and 'The Musician'.—C. S. P.*]

7

THE LITURGIST

by the Rev. Dom Gregory Dix, O.S.B.

enerosos animos labor nutrit, wrote Seneca, and the reverse is also true. It is only such spirits who can toil laboriously without being choked with the mere dust of scholarship. Walter Frere was *generosus* in the wide meanings of that noble word, both as a man and as a scholar. His natural capacities were exceptional, but they were fructified by a life-long discipline of study more arduous than might have been suspected from his apparent ease of production. It revealed itself in an immense accumulation of dated note-books, beginning (if I remember rightly) in 1889 and continuing in unbroken series to the year before his death. Each was filled with facts gathered from all sorts of sources, noted always in the same exquisite hand that seemed never to have been immature, never to have been hurried, that was never less regular and beautiful until a waver appeared two years or so before he died. When I was invited to examine them after his death, to decide which should be kept, it was impressive to understand how long and how painfully that swift mind—aware of its own 'weakness for the quick theory', as he once confessed—had sought to discipline itself by the plodding, grinding control of evidence.

In the first two note-books the interests were almost wholly historical, those of a student mastering for the first time the specialist's outline of his chosen 'period'—in Frere's case the ecclesiastical history of Tudor England. There were lists

121

of bishops in various key-years, each with the dates of his consecration and vacation of his see, brief biography and notes of his opinions, many with careful references to the original documentary records where further information was available; there were analyses of Statutes and Orders in Council; notes on official procedures, the names and character of legal officials, and so forth. It was a complete reconstruction of the machinery of Tudor ecclesiastical administration. But even among this collection of the mere tools of a 'prentice historian, he had had an eye for details that could illuminate the 'background', especially—as was natural—for small points of the liturgical history of the time. Quite early in the 90's the proportion of these liturgical *memoranda* steadily increased, and well before 1900 the strictly historical notes had almost ceased to be taken. What had been a secondary interest had become the main field of study.

Thenceforward the note-books were filled with an astonishing variety of *liturgica*, mostly of a very technical character. All scholars use note-books, of course, but few I think quite in Frere's way. Nearly every volume contained one or two miscellaneous collections of facts and references set down always neatly but quite disconnectedly, just as they were encountered. A year or two later some of them would reappear in a fresh note-book, sifted and set in connexion with new-found facts bearing on the same topic, with references to what already existed in print about the subject. This happened in some cases four or five times, until a little sketch of the whole subject had taken shape, in the middle, often, of a note-book ostensibly devoted to something else. This was repeated and revised and added to year after year, until it was ready for the direct preparation for publication, a stage which was done outside the note-books and of which scarcely any relics remained among Frere's papers. In several cases the material took twenty years or more to reach the press from the time when the subject first caught his interest. It was, I am sure, this long maturing of his matter which was the secret of Frere's distinguished style—terse but never abrupt,

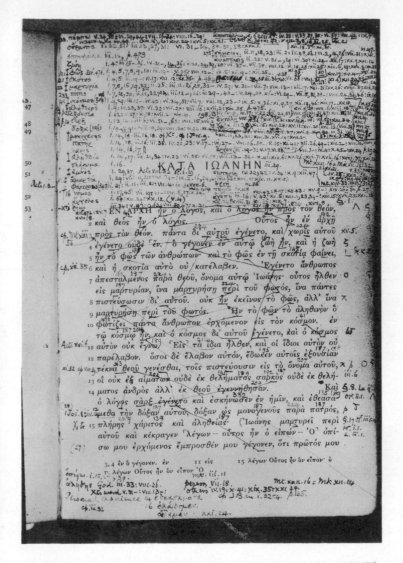

A PAGE OF W.H.F.'s MARKED GREEK TESTAMENT

pointed and vivid and using often what Henry James called 'the right word—I mean the intellectually surprising word', which yet exactly states. And always his writing is coolly lucid. Everything had been weighed and pondered again and again in that long distilling through the note-books, until in the end the actual work of preparation went easily enough, and the thought was clear and ready for that delicately austere style.

I well remember after his death examining at Mirfield sheet after sheet—there must have been thirty or forty of them—of incredibly neat columns of figures and symbols on squared paper, which looked at first sight like cryptograms. They represented what his fellow-scholars will probably always account Frere's greatest technical achievement, his investigation of the early history of the Roman Gospel and Epistle Lectionaries. The first was dated, I think, in 1898. Year by year, as successive summer holidays carried him to fresh Continental libraries, the materials grew and were elaborated, being set down almost every year in a fresh table incorporating the new discoveries. The system of the tables was complicated though very ingenious. Once one had discovered from the final printed account of the whole matter in Vols. II and III of his *Studies in the Early Roman Liturgy* (published only in 1934–5) what it was all about, it was fascinating to follow in the dated sheets each stage of the investigation as it had been carried out, and to watch the results of this intricate piece of research slowly taking shape over more than thirty years. The remarkable thing is that all the clues to the meaning of these complicated sheets must have been carried in his head from year to year, for there were no other *memoranda* of any kind. The drawback is seen in the fact that there still exists another collection of such sheets, representing a parallel investigation into the history of the Roman *Responsoriale*. This also had been brought to the final stage. But the book was never written, and in default of the clues to the symbols employed several examinations by some of those most familiar with Frere's methods of work have failed to make top or tail of them. It is to be feared that the material, so patiently gathered and sifted over so many years, may never be utilizable.

It was the existence of these large stocks of 'raw material' gathered in the 1900's which made possible the steady output of technical scholarship of a high order that distinguished Frere among the English bishops of the last thirty years. Some of his brother-bishops had been scholars before they were consecrated; one or two returned to scholarship, like Charles Gore, after resignation. But no other bishop that I recollect has found time for continuous scholarly production while he adorned the bench, as Lightfoot and Westcott and Wordsworth and Benson had contrived to do. Frere administered his diocese carefully and took his share in the councils of the bench in London. But he had the advantage that he did not come to the episcopate altogether without experience of the business of a great ecclesiastic. As Superior of Mirfield he had learned enough of the distractions from the world of books and ideas which must beset the scholar harnessed to administration to be able to avoid some of their most limiting effects. As a bishop, what had been his occupation had perforce become something of a hobby, but it was pursued steadily and with the same methods so far as duty permitted.

Most important, perhaps, he never lost his interest in and taste for technical scholarship under the burden of episcopal routine. He loved to talk of it, not merely to 'talk books' as any well-read man may do, but to 'talk scholarship' and of the *minutiae* that form its fascination and its discipline, and are the tools of the trade with which its large results upon the mind of the next generation are really wrought. When in London he was apt to forsake the Church Assembly and even the Upper House of Convocation in their drearier stretches for the Manuscript Room of the British Museum, with what sometimes looked very like relief. I was often working there at the time, and he would send me a note the day before asking me to get out against his coming particular books or MSS. The editions he wanted and the authors' names and often the Catalogue numbers would be stated precisely, drawn from the note-books; and he always knew exactly what it was that he wanted to study in each. He could no longer afford time to browse or to explore. He was intent only on completing and using the knowledge already gained.

I chance to have turned out recently a note from him written in 1929, asking me to have ready for him an article by Kekelidze in an obscure Russian periodical published in Tiflis in 1908. I remember that it cost me some trouble to get hold of it, partly because I could not read Russian and partly through the perversities of the heading 'Academies' in the old B.M. Catalogue, and when he came I was curious to know what he wanted with it. He had a twenty-year-old note, culled from a footnote in a quite different (German) periodical, that Kekelidze had there given a Russian translation of an old Georgian version of a still older Greek translation of the Canon of the Roman Mass, which contained an invoca- of the Holy Ghost in the *Te igitur*. He was hot-foot after 'the primitive Roman *epiklesis*'. We examined it together, he translating for me to copy. It required no long study to convince us both that this *epiklesis* was a late and foreign interpolation into the text of the old Latin prayer. Frere did not conceal his disappointment. I drew his attention to the odd fact that the interpolation was drawn not from the invocations of the Byzantine or Armenian liturgies, but *verbatim* from the Egyptian *Liturgy of St. Mark*. Here was a Roman prayer in a Caucasian church with an African addition! It gave one a startling little glimpse into the unknown liturgical cross-currents of the Dark Ages. Frere said wryly, 'Yes! It's all very disturbing. But this is no use to me'—and turned to work at something else. The investigation was intended for his book on *The Anaphora*, which appeared nine years later. But there is no trace of it there, for the result hardly suited its thesis. The curious will find the use he did make of it in *Studies in Early Roman Liturgy*, I, p. 58, where the 'disturbing' implications are ignored. He never forgot or wasted an acquired fact, but he could not always let facts master him.

WALTER HOWARD FRERE

The long period over which his publications extended and their steady flow make it an impossible task in a short essay to comment on all his writings without turning it into a mere catalogue. Many of them, too, are not of great permanent interest except to us who knew him, for he wrote much for the occasion—little pamphlets and papers contributed to current discussions on the practicalities of Anglican life and worship. Invariably written with knowledge and deftness, they all set out persuasively a personal policy and standpoint in 'Church politics' which is very consistent. But the particular urgencies in these things change a good deal from decade to decade, and such contributions lose their actuality. Some of the best of these *opera minora* have been collected by Dr. J. H. Arnold and E. G. P. Wyatt, Esq., in the Memorial Volume issued by the Alcuin Club (*A. C. Collections, XXXV*), which happily rescues from oblivion some characteristic little essays contributed by the Bishop to the *Truro Diocesan Gazette*. Its publication was a deserved and fitting tribute from a Society to which Frere had given much time and interest for many years, and to which as President his name had lent prestige.

I shall therefore confine myself here to those works of Bishop Frere with which his name will be permanently associated in the record of English scholarship. His earliest publications, *Memorials of Stepney Parish*, and *A Sketch of the Parochial History of Barley, Herts*, are alluded to in another chapter, and are in any case immature and of little interest. But with his next work, *The Winchester Troper* (H.B.S. 1894) he had entered suddenly into his proper field of study, the history of the liturgy, more particularly of English medieval liturgy. The change in the quality of the work is striking. There is the precision of style and that trick of clear exposition of complicated technical matters which never left him henceforward. He was also fully master of his subject. The practice of 'troping'—that is of interpolating liturgical texts with irrelevant phrases to assist their musical rendering—is not, perhaps, of any far-reaching significance or practical interest in liturgy. Even in its hey-day, it was rather a typical symptom of the medieval decadence of liturgical principles than a healthy development. But the practice was once wide-spread in the North and West of Europe, it had interesting historical ramifications and musical repercussions. Frere's investigation of the Winchester *répertoire* of tropes included a minute comparison with other Norman and English collections, and led up to a clarification of the whole history and geography of the subject. The little that has come to light since he wrote has only illustrated the conclusions which he reached fifty years ago. For a beginner in a science thus to exhaust his topic is unusual. In the same year appeared the first volume of his admirable edition of the *Sarum Gradual* for the Plainsong and Medieval Music Society, accompanied by a dissertation which showed no little specialized knowledge for that day of its more important and ancient source, the *Antiphonale Missarum* of St. Gregory, though later work has rather 'dated' some things in this part of the book.

This deeply-informed attention to the music which was an integral element (not accompaniment) of the medieval rites he studied was inherent in Frere's conception of the duty of a student of liturgy. Its value is well illustrated, for instance, in his paper on 'The Newly-found York Gradual' contributed to the *Journal of Theological Studies* in 1901, where it brings to life the essential scientific use of the new document in the study of liturgy, and translates it from the category of mere historical curiosity. Nor was this sense of the essential relation of music to worship confined in any way to the majestic tradition of the classical Church music of the West. It was extended just as sympathetically and with the same awareness to popular hymnody, witness his introduction to the *Historical Edition of Hymns Ancient and Modern*.

His connexion with the publications of the Alcuin Club began in 1899 with his edition of a fifteenth-century *Exposition de la Messe*, and continued for nearly forty years. But down to the issue of the first volume of his *Studies in Early Roman Liturgy*, on *The Kalendar*, in 1930, these were all of minor importance, though in all of them there is evidence of the care which he lavished on everything that he wrote.

Of permanent interest there appeared in this period his editions of *The Sarum Consuetudinary* and *The Ordinal and Tonal* (1898 and 1901), which established satisfactorily for the first time the relatively late compilation and French origin of a good deal which still passes for 'old English custom'— though this aspect of the matter is not unduly emphasized in Frere's account of it. It is an admirable edition of a text whose MS. sources were not without elements of complication. There is a good condensed Introduction, which rather conceals the amount of hard work which had gone into the making of the book. With this we may couple Frere's edition of the *Hereford Breviary* (H.B.S.) in collaboration with L. E. G. Brown. He began work on this in 1897 and it appeared in three volumes between 1904 and 1915. The move of his Community from Radley to Mirfield evidently caused difficulties and delays, for the originals from which Frere was working had been deposited by their custodians in the Bodleian for his study, and could not be moved with the editor-in-chief to Yorkshire. I should guess that the greater part of Vol. II is the work of Brown under Frere's occasional supervision. But the third is clearly almost entirely Frere's. It contains work which I should be inclined to select as perhaps the most characteristic of his best gifts and methods as a scholar that ever came from his hand (though that is not to say it is either the most important or the most interesting). The Introduction of sixty-eight pages is packed with information, set out with his enviably lucid condensation. There follow some additional Hereford texts illustrating the Breviary printed in Vols. I and II. At the end are 200 pages of Indices and Tables, all of the most beautiful accuracy. Frere loved making 'Tables'—probably because it is the briefest and simplest way of conveying detailed information for those who know how to use them, though it is a little hard on the wayfaring man. Already his *Winchester Troper* and *Sarum Gradual* and *Antiphoner* had shewn his fondness for them, and he was still using them skilfully in volumes published after his retirement. His own works were full of them. What to most researchers is not much better than a particularly laborious part of the drudgery which pays heavily for the humane pleasure of their vocation, had for him a special fascination which he was at no pains to repress. Those in Vol. III of the *Hereford Breviary* contain not only a complete *conspectus* of the whole text of the Divine Office in the use of Hereford, but also a minute comparison of every part of it with the uses of Sarum and York. The whole Secular Office of the Medieval English Church is analysed in these rather forbidding pages, a convenience nowhere else available to the serious student, and all done with a lovely accuracy. How many hours of unregarded monotonous labour it must have cost him I would not care to estimate.

In 1902 appeared what is still his best-known and most widely-used work—*A New History of the Book of Common Prayer*—familiar to all ordinands for forty years past as 'Procter and Frere'. On the basis of a rather clumsy old *History* by Canon Procter, Frere produced what he rightly called 'A New History', for it was largely rewritten and quite rejuvenated. A good deal of his own work *ex ipsis fontibus* on the Tudor and Stuart periods went into it, and the matter old and new was all set out in Frere's most engaging style. It took at once the place it still deserves to hold as the standard introduction to the subject, though more recent work will necessitate a recasting of some parts of it. What is of more importance here is that it was in a sense Frere's confession of faith as an Anglican churchman. More by its assumptions and selected standpoint than by direct statement, he here set out once for all his view of English Church History and of Church doctrine—as a 'Catholicism' which was not only justified but rather strictly limited by the historic Anglican formularies. He had had precursors, of course, in the seventeenth century and later, though he differed more than he perhaps realized from some of the nineteenth-century Tractarians like Pusey, as well as from some contemporary scholars like

Darwell Stone and Armitage Robinson, in the *rationale* of his theology. It was a view which he seems to have held before his ordination, in which he was partly confirmed by Bishop Gore, and to which he remained substantially faithful to the end, though in later years he came to admit more readily that it was not without some serious difficulties and limitations. But by and large he held to it unswervingly, and at bottom probably rather passionately, in spite of them. It is still a legitimate view, though it has probably now fewer upholders who are in the first rank of scholarship than in his own generation. But it was Frere's view, or rather his conviction, exceptionally strongly held, and it accounts for much in what he did and wrote—including an element of 'advocacy' in some of his writing which has been much criticized by scholars. But Frere was never afraid of being dubbed an 'advocate' where his convictions were involved, and it must be acknowledged that at least he could be a consummate one, advancing his case with a graceful reasonableness which seemed to palliate even his occasionally masterful handling of the evidence. His general thesis about 'Churchmanship' was something much deeper in the man even than a high and chivalrous loyalty; it was the foundation and central support of the life of a singularly holy priest, which he could never lose sight of in anything which he did or wrote. As such it must just be accepted and understood in an account of his scholarship. And I know of no writing anywhere in which that view is set out with more charm than in his revision of Procter's *History of the Book of Common Prayer*.

Another old book which he launched on a new life was Rock's *Church of our Fathers* (edited in collaboration with Fr. Hart, in 4 vols., 1904–5). Daniel Rock was a Roman Catholic priest and ecclesiastical antiquary of some note in the mid-nineteenth century, whose passionate love for the Anglo-Saxon and Medieval English Church touched Frere's own *pietas* closely. In this case the queer 'picturesque' English of the Pugin period in which Rock had chosen to write had to be reprinted without change. It would have been impossible to adapt this perfect 'period piece' without wholesale rewriting. Only a brief appendix of corrections to Vol. IV notes some points on which the work was now quite obsolete. What was completely revised by the editors was the large collection of passages from original sources and the illustrations, in which a great part of the book's value had always lain. Better texts and a much wider array of authorities in the new edition witnessed not only to the immense advance in English medieval studies—in which Rock had been something of a pioneer—made since his day, but also to the width and particularity of Frere's own knowledge in this field.

The volume of his publications lessened with his re-election as Superior of the growing Community at Mirfield, but there are two pieces of work, the one continued and the other wholly completed during this period, of which something must be said. The one is his *Bibliotheca Musico-Liturgica* (1901 and 1932). He was evidently occupied at intervals with work on the second volume. Of all his books I think 'my Bibliotheca', as he called it, was secretly his darling. Like so many of them it was *un œuvre de longue haleine*, taking a whole generation to complete. It was intended to be a complete descriptive catalogue of all the medieval liturgical MSS. extant in English libraries, and it was not so far from fulfilling that large ambition. A few slips in the catalogue numbers of MSS. witness to the impossibility of verifying notes hurriedly made twenty or thirty years before in libraries which he had never been able to revisit; and a certain amount of material—mostly of more interest on the musical than on the liturgical side—has come to light since he worked. But it is still the standard work of reference in this field, and will never be displaced in its value to all serious students of the subject. To Frere's own studies of medieval English liturgy the unique knowledge of what still actually exists in unpublished MSS. with which this survey equipped him, added an exceptional solidity and authority.

The other piece of work wholly carried out while still Superior was his essay on 'Early Forms of Ordination' in the volume of *Essays on the Early History of the Church and Ministry*, edited by H. B. Swete (1918). Frere was a little on the defensive about this essay, and it must be acknowledged that it has been not so much criticized as dismissed by specialists. I think this was inevitable in the circumstances. From the point of view of the progress of knowledge of the subject the volume as a whole was not opportune. The work of Hatch and Harnack in the 'eighties had raised a group of entirely new problems in the field of Early Church Order, which were none of them yet ripe for a solution. Even the materials for the needed reconstruction of Lightfoot's theory were not yet all available, let alone understood, and a pause of a decade or more after that would have been natural for their assimilation in a right perspective, before anything so definitive as this volume sought to be should have been attempted. But its production had been virtually commanded by Archbishop Davidson in 1911 for reasons of ecclesiastical policy—an art whose preoccupations do not always coincide with what is desirable for the advancement of learning. Swete's words in the Introduction, 'The reader will find that few facts emerge from the enquiry of which no account had been taken previously', apply to Frere's essay as well as to most of the others. They could not have been written if it had been postponed for ten or twelve years. The authors were quite aware of the difficulties and not too eager to encounter them. Turner and Brightman were both five years [*sic*] late in sending in their contributions, and (so Armitage Robinson once told me) they were all so discouraged by the circumstances that the essayists agreed that it was not worth while to meet even once for a common examination of the problems. It is not surprising, therefore, that of the six essays in the book, though all were by scholars of the very first order, only that of Robinson still retains most of its value. Even Turner's great contribution on 'Apostolic Succession' now requires some re-handling.

Frere's essay seems to have been written in 1912–13 and to have been hurriedly revised in 1916. It is chiefly concerned with what he calls 'this puzzling heap of literature', the so-called 'Church Orders'——a group of closely inter-related Christian documents of the third and fourth centuries. Their true connexions and affiliations were first satisfactorily demonstrated by Dom R. H. Connolly in *The So-called Egyptian Church Order* (Cambridge, October 1916), which appeared only in time to be mentioned in Frere's concluding footnote. It is true that when he wrote Frere had the advantage of acquaintance with the pamphlet *Über die pseudo-apostolischen Kirchenordnungen* of E. Schwartz (Strasbourg 1910), in which the right solution of the puzzles had been cursorily sketched. Incidentally, Frere must have been almost the only scholar in England who had then read it; even Connolly was unaware of it when writing his own larger and more satisfactory study. I remember Frere telling me, 'It was the Dean' (Armitage Robinson) 'who put me on to that. He had always read everything before other people had heard of it.' But Schwartz had dealt with the questions which specially concerned Frere only incidentally, and partly by way of somewhat lofty assumptions. Frere evidently hesitated to commit himself finally to the German scholar's conclusions, even though his argument follows broadly the same lines. The confusion in the essay which results from this hesitation between the new and right solutions and the desire to leave open a line of retreat to the old theory of Achelis and Harnack which was then still in possession of the field, robs Frere's argument of some of its usual ease and lucidity, and——it must be admitted——of most of its value for time to come. There are other unsatisfactory features. A discovery of Turner's, published in 1915, is awkwardly incorporated on p. 284, evidently in the process of revision, which really necessitated a more drastic revision of the preceding ten pages. The nomenclature adopted for the various documents is designedly vague and colourless to avoid begging questions; but this involves obscuring important implications of the evidence which arise precisely from the facts of date and *provenance* which Frere had to leave on one side as uncertain. It also partly conceals the fact that Frere is working to some extent from his own hypothetical 'reconstructions' of the earliest redactions of the documents, rather than from the extant documents themselves. That his 'reconstructions' have now turned out to be much more right than wrong amply vindicates his good judgment. But this could not add to the probative force of his essay when it appeared, or increase his reputation with contemporary scholars.

It was unfortunate that this should have been his only major contribution on the special problems of early Christian literature, in which he took a continuous, informed and penetrating interest. The truth is that no scholar in Europe could have handled these particular topics satisfactorily at the stage which knowledge had then reached. Frere's essay is a relic of a tentative period, but when that handicap is borne in mind its value appreciates considerably. Not only does it make livelier reading than most of the literature about the Church Orders—that would not be difficult. But having recently completed a very similar piece of work with the much ampler resources now available, I am in a position to say that it contains many acute and original observations on particular points in the documents which only the true scholar's instinct would have marked. For these it is still well worth reading by those who have mastered the more modern treatment of the subject.

The completion of E. S. Dewick's edition of *The Leofric Collectar* for the Henry Bradshaw Society (Vol. II, 1921) was the only other major piece of work he was able to finish before he was called from Mirfield to be Bishop of Truro. There can be little doubt that, though he had many gifts of soul and mind that indicated an eminent fitness for the episcopate, it was his liturgical learning which weighed most heavily with Archbishop Davidson when he pressed this appointment of the first Religious to the Anglican bench since the sixteenth century. The tortuous business of Prayer Book revision had been in progress (if that be the word) ever since 1906, and had drifted into a more expansive phase after the first

World War. A bench of bishops wholly innocent of technical knowledge of what it was about was finding itself in growing difficulties as its projects grew more ambitious. Frere was the obvious man to give competent guidance in the more thoroughgoing revision now in prospect. He had steeped himself in the historic tradition of Anglican worship as well as in its wider background in antiquity and the Latin Middle Ages; he was the author of what had now been recognized for twenty years as the standard Anglican book on the subject; many of his lesser writings had witnessed to a deliberate and lengthy preparation of his gifts for this special task. What was perhaps more to the Archbishop's mind, Frere had associated himself whole-heartedly with the project of revision, whereas most 'Anglo-Catholics'—on whom the blame for any need of revision at all was officially cast— were manifesting an obstinate suspicion of the whole business, in view of the 'police' aspects of the projected new liturgy which some of the bishops were incautiously advertising. But for Frere it was his hour on Pisgah after forty years of expectation.

It is a little difficult to write of what followed, because it concerned Walter Frere the great ecclesiastic quite as much as Walter Frere the scholar; and the embers of the disputes kindled among Churchmen in 1927–8 are still hot in the minds of some of the older among us, for whom his name remains something of a battle-cry, for and against, in these things. I think that the truth is that the time has not yet come for a final assessment of his share either in the actual process of revision or in the events that followed, because the exact facts are not yet fully known. Some things there are, however, which can already be said.

The late Bishop T. B. Strong of Oxford compiled in 1928 what seems likely to be the only full account of the long series of 'secret' discussions held by the bishops at Lambeth. It is now deposited under seal, with an instruction that it is not to be published before a certain date. (Having read some parts of it at Cuddesdon before it was so sepulchred, and listened to Strong reciting others, I may be allowed to say that this seems to me just as well. It is a document not without passages of the naughty wit of which that shy prelate was capable. There was one discussion about eucharistic Prefaces and 'the Tune', in which Strong mimicked the voices of some of the bishops and the tone of Frere's incisive comments in reply——! And there were others which may damage some reputations, though their possessors will by then be only names to the reader.) It is clear that the difficulties Frere encountered in explaining liturgical matters to his brethren were unexpectedly great, and that some of them were depressing, where they were not ludicrous, to one who understood so well the subject in hand. Almost single-handed he prevented the inclusion of more than one quite grotesque proposal in the episcopal draft, to some of which their pained authors clung with a pathetic energy. There can be no question that from this aspect Frere's inclusion in the counsels of the bishops was of the greatest value.

On his positive contribution opinions can differ. He was convinced that the English Church had come to a parting of the ways in eucharistic theology, that henceforward it was bound either increasingly to follow the contemporary 'Anglo-Catholic' trend towards the medieval Western view and practice, or else, if this was to be avoided, a corrective must be brought in both in liturgy and theology from the Oriental tradition. (In point of fact there seems to have been a third line of evolution which he never envisaged, but which may perhaps be that on which *Ecclesia Anglicana* will ultimately set out.) His own sympathies had been strongly drawn towards the East by his intercourse with Orthodox, and especially Russian, theologians, and he was sure that the moment had come for giving a decisive turn Eastwards to the Anglican development.

He justified his opinions then and later by a view of early liturgical history which he supported with all the resources of his learning, though it has since failed to gain much support from the consensus of scholarly opinion, as it failed at the time to win the assent of men of the calibre of Brightman and Armitage Robinson. At bottom, I believe the view which he held arose first of all out of what he considered healthy for the future development of Anglicanism, rather than from what presented itself to him from patristic and liturgical study. But he certainly put it before the bishops as primarily a thesis about primitive eucharistic doctrine and practice, and they seem to have been almost entirely unaware that as such it was open to much expert question. The proposed new Canon of 1927-8 was the general result of the impact of Frere's theory on the minds of the bishops, though he by no means had things all his own way in the details of the drafting. He was not himself the author of the phrasing of the *Epiklesis*, on which so much controversy subsequently turned, and he was prepared in private conversation to criticize it somewhat drastically. But he accepted it as being sufficient for the ultimate purpose he had in mind, and campaigned vigorously for its adoption. At one stage, in 1926, he went so far as to 'block' a proposal for its optional use, though by 1928 he had been converted to the necessity of this. His ideas had, too, a considerable influence on the final form of other parts of the eucharistic liturgy, though some, whose adoption would have given a much better finish to the workmanship of the rite, he was unable to persuade the other bishops to accept. But it would be a misrepresentation if I were to suggest that in 1927-8 he regarded either the 'Deposited Book' itself or its *epigonon* of the next year as anything like the ideal rite of his own hopes. He then spoke of both in terms of some disappointment, though he certainly advocated the first as preferable to the book of 1662.

His mind on both is given as fully as need be by the following letter, in answer to Canon Cooper, then the Chancellor of his cathedral:

Lis Escop, Truro,
14*th March* 1928.

My dear Chancellor,

Your letter asks me to comment on the present position of

the Prayer Book revision and especially of the changes recently recommended by the Houses of Clergy and Laity. Frankly I think it improper to introduce any changes of substance at this last stage: and I think, as you do, that these new recommendations are likely (if adopted by the bishops) to make things worse and not better.

I supported the Deposited Book which the Assembly approved but the House of Commons rejected. It contained, besides a number of things which I merely disliked, one or two things which seemed to me not only unwise but unjust. However, in the hope that it might serve, at any rate for the time, as a basis of peaceful and orderly administration in matters of worship, I supported it.

The Deposited Book has now been altered by all three Houses of the Church Assembly and these alterations have cut away the ground of my support. I see now no sufficient hope of settlement, but on the contrary the prospect of acute trouble.

You will not expect me to go into so voluminous a subject at any length: but I will try to indicate very briefly some of the chief points of my indictment.

1. In the directions concerning the Holy Communion the Houses of Clergy and Laity have demanded an insertion which I think revolutionary. Hitherto the initiative and first responsibility about services has rested on the shoulders of the Parish Priest: the Parochial Church Council has been given a formal right of protest; and in case of discord the Bishop is invoked to arbitrate and decide. The new demand is that the Council should be able to issue a certain command to the Priest, apart from the Bishop, which he must thereupon carry out. That some provision should be made for communicants who desire the rite of 1662 is, of course, desirable: but the already existing method of securing this by joint action of Priest and People (and Bishop if needed) was adequate. This new provision is an insult to the Clergy and a snub to the Bishops.

2. I am personally well satisfied with the new Canon: but,

being so, I am the more concerned for the large body of those who are not, both Evangelicals and Anglo-Catholics. The Roman type of liturgy has prevailed in the English Church from St. Augustine's time till now: and I think it is unfair that no suitable form of Canon should be provided for those who wish to keep that type, or who for other reasons mislike an *Epiklesis*. Peace and contented worship can hardly be secured while the desire of so large a class of worshippers is refused.

3. The subject of fasting in general and of the fast before communion in particular is a large one. It calls for fresh investigation, so far as the relation of past custom to present conditions is concerned, and probably for some reconstruction and restatement. But such needed handling of the matter will be only hindered by the adoption in the form of a rubric, of any such brief statement as is desired by the Houses of Clergy and Laity. Besides this, the seriousness and adequacy of preparation for communion (difficult enough to secure in any case) would necessarily be impaired by any such rubric, even if it did not take the outrageous form suggested, of saying in effect that it is as good to break with Catholic custom as to observe it. Such a line is clean contrary to the tradition of the English Church.

4. Lastly, with regard to the Reservation of the Blessed Sacrament, there has been during the closing stages of the revision a sad faltering in the spirit of generosity and trust which once prevailed; this has led, step after step, to the accumulation of a mass of rigid restrictions. The Parish Priest in his pastoral office is tied up too tight, the Bishop as Administrator is fettered, and the Laity have their privileges unfairly curtailed.

(*a*). I know of no justification for rigidly confining the benefit to the sick. Administration to the whole would no doubt need regulation; but it is unfair to make it impossible for persons who are debarred from coming regularly at the times of service. Besides, it is, surely, very undesirable that the Sacrament reserved should be isolated from all communion given in the church, and so from the idea of communion.

(*b*). For the purpose of reservation is communion. This primary purpose, however, does not preclude advantages secondary and incidental. These should be recognized and even taken to some extent into account in determining the places where reservation is licensed. The restrictions in the Deposited Book were too narrow; but these which are now put forward are worse and will soon be found impracticable.

Reflecting, therefore, on the present position, and passing over many minor matters, I reluctantly realize that we tend to hinder Communion, to depreciate the Holy Eucharist, to discourage a valued form of prayer, to decry fasting, to subjugate the Parish Priests to their Councils, to hamper Episcopal Administration, besides ignoring a legitimate claim for another form of Canon.

I regret to say that I have little hope that the final decisions of the Bishops will be found, when they appear, to remedy these defects: and in this case I shall be unable to vote in Convocation for sending the measure on to the Assembly.

Yours affectionately,
WALTERUS TRURON.

Certainly this 'indictment' is not the language of enthusiasm, and the reasons which he gives for his support even of the Deposited Book of 1927 are those of a statesman rather than of a liturgical scholar. He carried out his intention of voting against going forward with the 1928 book at all. That he subsequently reacted sharply again, and became the strongest promoter of the ecclesiastical use of the book which he had rejected, is well known and has puzzled many people, though he himself once wrote to me, 'I am conscious of no palinode.'

Looking back, I think his change of attitude was due to three main motives, which were all present to his mind, though I cannot assess the relative weight of them with him. The first was a deep disdain for the tactics of the campaign in the 'Protestant underworld' which was responsible for the second defeat of the Revision in Parliament. He found it difficult to be just to the conscientious motives which had inspired the 'handful of octogenarians' who 'generalled' it. The second was his unwillingness to accept the total frustration of what had for him been the cherished hope of a lifetime. He had desired revision for forty years in the interests of a truer and fuller worship. Its defeat came to seem to him a damaging blow to the interests of religion as such in the Church of England. Thirdly, he recognized much sooner than did most of his brother-bishops the serious consequences of disintegration likely to arise in the inner life of the Church from the policy they officially adopted, of declining to accept the decision of Parliament as binding and yet refraining from trying to rally the Church whole-heartedly behind the use of the new book as the primary Anglican instrument of worship. The truth is that its chief interest for most of them lay in its restrictive regulations, while for him it lay in the new Canon, viewed simply as a prayer. In his advocacy of the 1928 book it was this which he was really trying to save from the wreck, and for its sake he swallowed as best he could a number of other things in the book which had originally seemed to him so repellent as to decide him to vote against it altogether. He always declared that the objectionable features would prove quite unworkable in practice and would have to be dropped, if only people would adopt the book. In point of fact some of them have persisted as episcopal norms of administration ever since, while the prayer he desired for its own sake has not been generally adopted.

Whether his was in truth a more realistic policy than that of the other bishops is not for me to say. It now seems very doubtful whether the book of 1928 would ever have aroused much enthusiasm in the Church as a whole, even with much more decided episcopal support. But, as it was, the bishops certainly contrived to make the worst of both worlds, and it is conceivable that by taking Frere's course they might have

placed themselves in a better position to control the subsequent liturgical diversity and in a further ten years time to
give that more constructive lead to the Church for which
Frere still hoped. But *episcopi Angliæ semper pavidi* was not a
new discovery even in the days of St. Anselm, and has been
sufficiently consistently followed ever since to be accounted
almost a principle of continuity. They shrank from the possibility of widening the breach with the State and the ultimate
disestablishment which such a course might entail. Frere
both spoke and wrote of them as 'feeble'.

He continued to lead his forlorn hope with a gallant per-
sistence, even when it became obvious that the Church at
large was not going to follow him. As time passed and his
disappointment grew, it would occasionally break out in wry
remarks. It was then—about 1929—that he formed the idea
of making a supreme attempt to justify not the 1928 book
as a whole but the 1928 Canon, by a book on eucharistic
theology as expressed in the liturgy of the Early Church. Its
composition was much hampered by ill-health, but it appeared eventually in 1938, a few weeks before his death, as
The Anaphora.

He sent me an advance copy as 'a target offered rather
fearfully to you and your heavy artillery'. We had discussed
the book and its thesis several times, once for a whole hot
afternoon and evening on the lawn at Lis Escop. It had
seemed to me then that he was being rather cavalier with the
evidence, and that his case rested on several unproved—and
(as it appeared to me) unlikely—assumptions; and he had admitted then and since that his case was 'difficult'. I must confess that I read it for the first time in print with some dismay.
It was not so much the thesis, with which I was familiar, or
even the petulance with which it was in a few places expressed.[1] There were flashes of the old intense feeling for

[1] It is right to say here that two or three phrases, the only bitter or unjust
words which ever appeared from his pen, greatly troubled the Bishop when
he encountered them in page-proof. He was anxious to eliminate them from
the book, but the publishers, who had already cited them in a widely circulated
advertisement, refused to allow him to change them. The authorities of the

the sense of words, and stretches of the old lucidity. But there were other things also—sentences without main verbs, occasional false references and mistranslations—things which Frere as I had last seen him only four months before would never have let pass. The proofs had evidently been corrected for the press by a very sick man. He wrote again two days later pressing me for my criticisms and I replied, unwillingly, with a sketch of some points in the evidence which he seemed to me to have failed to take into account. He answered again in a shaky hand:

Yours will not be the only criticisms. You must publish this.

> '*Shoot sharp, love, and spare not.*
> *Spend thy bolts; I care not:*
> *fal la la la la la la!*'

if I may mangle an Elizabethan: only with *me*, 'care not' = 'resent not': for care I shall, to have your heaviest and lightest word. Accept the book with my love.

Your affect.
WALTER FRERE, C.R.

A week later, when I chanced to be staying for the night at the Mirfield Priory in London, I received the telephoned news that he had just died. I felt as I had not felt since the death of my own father.

It would be unjust to Walter Frere's great reputation as a scholar to end upon the mention of this book. The real crown of his life's work was his *Studies in Early Roman Liturgy*, in which his gifts shone undimmed and his judgment was at the peak of maturity. They appeared in three volumes: I, *The Kalendar*; II, *The Gospel Lectionary*; III, *The Epistle Lectionary*; and the Alcuin Club, for which he had done so many minor works, had the honour of publishing them. (As

Alcuin Club were informed after his death of his strong desire to omit them, but preferred to reprint them in their Memorial Volume as they appeared. I think I owe it to the Bishop's memory, for he was ever the most courteous of controversialists, to make these facts public.

has been said, there was to have been a fourth volume on the Responsories at the Night Office, but this was never completed, owing to his preoccupation with *The Anaphora* in the last year of his life.) The subject was intricate and highly specialized, and Frere had been mastering it for forty years. A few tiny slips mar the perfection of the first volume, but the other two are well-nigh flawless. They were received with a chorus of respectful admiration by the liturgical scholars of all Europe in the learned periodicals of the Continent, and they set a seal upon his whole life's labour of learning in a way which no publication of purely Anglican interest could have done.

It has not fallen to me to say much of the man, of his charm and his gaiety, and an exasperating way he had in argument of riding off on a weak case with a plea of 'other issues', and his radiant holiness and his wisdom about things that are not found in books. The adjective that always formed itself in my mind as I watched him was 'debonair'; it suited the tilt of his head and the peculiar, almost dancing, stance, and the untroubled courage with which I have seen him meet great sorrow and disappointment. I owe him more than I can say, not only for teaching, of which I am proud to speak, but also for affection, of which one does not speak. There were in him three men, the ecclesiastical statesman, the scholar and the man of God. And if, as it seemed to me, the statesman in him sometimes influenced the scholar, in the stress of the difficult business of being an English bishop, he never came near to influencing the great and holy priest that he was.

It is hard to sum up the work of a man one has revered, harder still to 'place' it accurately in its exact importance in the history of learning when one has been a disciple, even after eight years have given some perspective. Frere was of that remarkable group of Christian scholars—Armitage Robinson, Burkitt, Figgis, Abbot Butler, A. J. Mason, Swete—in whom (with Dom Connolly still happily surviving) Cambridge provided something of a succession in the true line to its even greater 'Trio' of the generation before them. That group made a mark of its own on the English scholarship of the first quarter of this century. The temper and the needs of the time have changed abruptly since then, and some of their high qualities no longer correspond exactly to the demands now made upon theology. But their breadth and humanity and their discrimination did much more than is always appreciated by my own contemporaries to carry English theological learning through the difficult period of theological disintegration in the 1900's, and through what was perhaps the still more difficult St. Martin's Summer of 'Liberalism' in the 1920's. Armitage Robinson was their *princeps*—though not so *facile*, but rather as the central star in a constellation than as a sun among planets. There were other luminaries, of course, Gore and Turner and others, but the Cambridge men in retrospect formed something of a group. To Robinson the others were apt to turn at times for guidance, more perhaps because of a sort of sure 'instinct' of sagacity which he had in the kind of questions they were all handling, than because of a greatly outstanding pre-eminence above the rest in intellectual gifts.

So, at least, I know that Frere regarded him. When he was Bishop of Truro he was summoned to be Robinson's priest upon his death-bed. Three days after the funeral he told me of it in the British Museum. 'The Dean was incorrigible; demanding cups of tea and asking "If I can't be a nuisance now, when shall I be able to be?" I found a copy of *The Didache* on the bed when I went to give him the last sacraments! I think that theory of his (as to the dependence of *The Didache* on the *Epistle of Barnabas*) will turn out to be right in the end. He had an instinct about these things.' But if Frere reverenced Robinson's quality as a scholar, it was characteristic of a complementary reverence which was always noticeable on 'the Dean's' side that the formidable old polymath turned to Frere at the end for the last great service that one priest can do another.

In the larger history of scholarship Frere's place is with the liturgists—distinguished company enough for any man.

They fall, I think, the eminent among them, into two groups, divided not by a degree of greatness, but by a diversity of gifts. There are those to whom their successors turn naturally for texts and 'information'—Bona, Eusébe Renaudot, Martène, the Blessed Tommasi, le Sieur de Moléon (of whose enchanting *Voyage Liturgique* Frere once gave me a copy he had picked up for a shilling), le Brun, Forbes, Wilson, Brightman, are names that occur. And there is another group—Mabillon, Claude de Vert, Probst, Ceriani, Edmund Bishop, Wilmart are representative—no less equipped with facts, but to whom one turns rather for their *aperçus*, their general judgments. These saw the liturgy always as a thing embedded deep in the passing history of Europe and the abiding life of the Church. The two groups overlap, of course. Mabillon and Wilmart for instance were great editors; Pierre le Brun and others had plenty of theories. But I believe that those who know the subject most profoundly will agree that it is to the one group that one turns instinctively for 'facts' and for 'information', to the other for 'judgments' and for 'understanding' (whether one's own judgment agrees with theirs or not).

It is with the first group that Frere's name will live. True, he had a foot in either camp. He has left us one finished piece of specialized research on the Roman Mass-lectionaries as near perfection as it is ever given to mortal man to reach, whose conclusions will remain magisterial in their own field. But he has left behind him a whole shelf of standard editions of texts. At the difficult and laborious task of editing he was superbly competent—exactly faithful and of an excellent judgment, shrinking from no labour of index and table and analysis, yet always scrupulous to let the document speak for itself. Failing the discovery of radically new material, which in this part of the field is no longer very probable, these editions of his will be definitive. For centuries to come all students of medieval English *liturgica* will approach many of their most important documents under the guidance of Walter Frere. And they will be grateful.

8

THE HISTORIAN

by A. Hamilton Thompson, C.B.E., D.Litt., LL.D., F.B.A.

Frere's reputation as a liturgiologist somewhat overshadows his distinction as an historian. While, however, it is possible, in contemplating his liturgical studies, to forget the basis on which they were founded, that basis was a wide and scholarly knowledge of ecclesiastical history and a special devotion to the duty of examining the history of the national Church. Convinced of its continuity at the most critical period of its existence, he brought to the proof of his conviction a keen intelligence and a gift of plain and candid statement which raised his work above the level of controversy and made it a source of reference, not merely for sympathizers, but for opponents who recognized his acquaintance with and skill in the interpretation of original documents. Students of his edition of Procter's *History of the Book of Common Prayer* know well the value of its contribution to the history of the Reformation in England and of the circumstances which directed the several steps in the progress of the Prayer Book to its present form. Both in that work and in such undertakings as his collaboration in revising Rock's *Church of our Fathers* his thorough acquaintance with historical sources is clearly visible, and not the least value of such volumes is the *catena* of pertinent quotations and references which their footnotes constantly supply.

His earliest published work was historical. More than one

bishop with the best intentions has encouraged his parochial
clergy in the study of local history as a useful occupation for
leisure hours; and, although the task has often been accompanied by an enthusiasm which has dispensed with sufficient
preparation or has allowed itself more leisure hours than are
compatible with parochial duties, the result of such advice
has been on the whole successful. It need hardly be said that
a mind so well trained and disciplined as that of Frere could
safely be trusted to exercise itself upon the records of Stepney, the historic parish in which for five years he served as an
assistant curate, and upon the main details of the story of a
familiar parish in Hertfordshire, without any risk of falling
into extremes of undue haste or excessive preoccupation with
his subject.

His entry into the Community of the Resurrection gave
him full opportunity for the type of study in which he excelled. While the recently-founded Henry Bradshaw Society
provided an appropriate outlet for his liturgical researches,
the Church Historical Society, under the energetic chairmanship of Forrest Browne, then Bishop of Stepney, gladly
availed itself of his services. In July 1895 this society issued
a circular inviting the bishops of the Church of England to
institute enquiries through their registrars or other competent persons into episcopal records of the time of Cardinal
Pole (1554–8), 'with a view to ascertaining whether there
are any indications of the acceptance of Orders conferred
according to the Edwardian rite'. Such enquiries meant the
employment of a trained enquirer who would collect information and report upon it. Frere's report was delivered to the
Committee of the Society and published in 1896 under the
title, *The Marian Reaction in its relation to the English Clergy.*
A list of 'books constantly quoted' shows, to any one
acquainted with such sources, how little had actually been
done with this particular object in view and what careful
investigation of episcopal records at first hand was necessary.
The fourth volume of R. W. Dixon's history, dealing with
the reign of Mary, was a recent publication indispensable for

purposes of reference, but the documentary evidence which it contained needed amplification. Frere thoroughly realized the drawbacks involved in his search, the imperfection of the registers for the material required and the consequent difficulty of forming general conclusions with complete accuracy. The book, however, which perhaps has never received the recognition which it fully deserves, is a very thorough and competent survey of a type of document which at the date in question had received but little attention, save from county historians compiling lists of incumbents of benefices and not unready to shirk the problems of this difficult period. Frere divided his work into five chapters. First, he treated of the Marian episcopate itself; secondly, he gave an account of the existing registers; thirdly, he dealt with evidence regarding deprivations of clergy; fourthly, with the evidence derived from records of ordinations; and, lastly, with the action of Pole as cardinal-legate. These chapters are followed by a long series of appendices containing the text or summaries of original documents from registers and elsewhere.

The result of the survey was far from positive, but it brought much to light that made any declaration of the invalidity of Edwardian Orders in the light of their rejection or of measures for it during the period extremely hazardous. Frere's desire that his work should demonstrate the practical possibility of a revision of the hostile view of Anglican Orders was disappointed at a later date by the uncompromising attitude of the bull *Apostolicæ Curæ*; but his book remains as a useful corrective to prejudice and a permanent witness to the weakness of the grounds on which opposition rested. For the historian it has no greater value than its clear statement of the nature of an episcopal register and its summary account of the information to be sought in its contents. The miscellaneous nature of such collections and frequent errors with regard to the limitations of documents in them make it perhaps easier to say what an episcopal register is not than what it is; but Frere went to his work fully armed, and to no mind was the danger of conjecture and of deductions which extend evidence beyond its due bounds more apparent. In 1899 had appeared the first volume of a general history of the English Church, edited by William Hunt and W. R. W. Stephens, two historians well tried in that special field. Eventually completed in eight volumes by various writers, this is still valued as an authority, and to none of its volumes is this reputation better due than to that by Frere. This, published in 1904, covered the reigns of Elizabeth and James I, a period in which temptations to stray from the path of strict impartiality abound, so tortuous and full of contradictions were the impulses of the age and the policies which they directed. The volume may be regarded as Frere's chief contribution to history, written soberly and clear-sightedly, with a sound appreciation of the true nature of the problems which beset the Church after the Marian interval, the danger involved by the zeal of returned exiles for the protestantism which they had imbibed at Continental centres, their mutual rivalries, the growing strength of puritanism with its risk of disruption, the repressed but vigorous activities of adherents of the Roman supremacy encouraged by the bull of excommunication and aided by the efforts of the newly-founded Society of Jesus. The story is familiar, with its record of wayward action which at times hindered progress and threatened spiritual growth: its end was but the beginning of a conflict which brought temporary disaster to the sorely-tried Church. Yet at no time did Frere allow his sympathies to run away with him; his calm judgment was awake to the sincerity and wisdom of the middle course which the Church steered between two extremes. He himself, pursuing that *via media* with assured tread, was able to regard these opposed points of view without partisan bitterness. The excesses of the puritan spirit can hardly be denied or even defended by its warmest admirers; but to its best representatives, even when, as in the case of Thomas Cartwright, real piety and zeal for religion were obscured by the mists of controversy, Frere was eminently fair. He was at pains to emphasize the best traits of a movement which was all the more dangerous in that it was carried on for a long period within the shelter of the Church to whose scheme of government it was hostile, while actively endeavouring to check developments of doctrine and ceremonial that competed with its cherished ideals. Puritanism to him had its place in the progress of English religion, and that no inconspicuous place, and he did not hesitate in showing his appreciation of its best qualities.

The passage in which he does this is one of those to which readers of the book will turn with interest as summing up the historian's attitude to the leading problems of his period. Equally interesting is his verdict upon the character and work of Archbishop Parker. The general estimate of Parker's activity has been somewhat subordinated to the perennial controversy with respect to his consecration and his consequent power of maintaining the continuity of episcopal government and demonstrating its reality as a channel through which the benefits of the Incarnation are conveyed to the children of the English Church. 'Nag's Head fables', arguments founded upon the absence of a record of Barlow's consecration which might have been applied with equal force to the absence of similar records at an earlier date, doubts of the authenticity of the evidence in Parker's register raised by zealots imperfectly acquainted with the nature and methods of composition of such a document, have all had their day and their sequels, and nothing indicates the fruitlessness of such attacks more clearly than the shifting character of the grounds on which they have been founded. Frere's acquaintance with historical documents, their forms and their limitations, enabled him to treat the controversial point without delaying over it. In the consecration of Parker we have a historical fact of supreme importance to the Church, and the essential question is, To what did it lead? There is no point of interest in Frere's work so arresting as his statement of what the English Church owes to the guidance of Parker, whose learning and conservative temperament, alive to the needs of the future and the risks they must bring, were yet capable of preserving the traditions of the past and demonstrating their compatibility with the course upon which the Church had entered.

His own tastes and temperament peculiarly fitted Frere to the special task of eulogizing Parker, with whose antiquarian pursuits and love of manuscripts he had all the sympathy of a careful scholar. Other personalities he perhaps found it more difficult to estimate so accurately; and with some, as with Grindal and Sandys, he had little in common. Whitgift's striking role in the history of his age is, again, not easy to qualify correctly, and puritan condemnation of a discipline which was undoubtedly severe and repressive, together with the resentment of papist recusants on whom it fell heavily, has done much to affect his reputation. Without minimizing or excusing his official rigour, however, save in so far as it was in keeping with the spirit of an age which knew nothing of the advantages of gentle and conciliating methods and would have profited little by their use, Frere brings out elements in his character and instances of clement action, modifying considerably the reputation of a relentless persecutor which, acutely pointed by the rough wit of the Marprelate tracts, has clung to the name of Whitgift. And, for the wisest, most saintly and most lovable of the Jacobean prelates, Lancelot Andrewes, Frere, cautious of displaying undue emotion, had nothing but sympathetic praise.

A word must be said of the style of the book, which admirably reflects the judicial and well-balanced qualities of mind of its author. He was the child of an age which had been alive to the literary responsibilities of the historian, somewhat overlooked perhaps at a later day, and had been marked by the conspicuous merits and individuality of more than one historical style. Frere aimed at nothing more than a 'serviceable' prose style which conveys what it has to say clearly and concisely, and the result is a complete success. Moreover, not only is the style clear, but Frere succeeded in being readable and consistently interesting: his own interest in his theme never flags and he had the gift of communicating it to the reader.

It is on this book that his reputation as an historian must principally rest, and, as time went on, he supplied students of the period with volumes of *pièces justificatifs*, edited with all the care and accuracy of ripe and finished scholarship. The three volumes of Articles and Injunctions contributed to the publications of the Alcuin Club, with an elaborate introduction, were prepared in collaboration with Mr. W. P. Kennedy, who continued the work later in three more volumes with the title *Elizabethan Church Administration*, supplied by the treatise contained in the first of the three. When in 1904 the Canterbury and York Society was founded for the publication of episcopal registers, Frere was one of the first members of Council. To him and to the skilled transcriber who worked under his guidance the Society owes its edition of Parker's register, a work which extended over many years. The fact that an editor so learned and so conscientious was found to undertake this formidable task should have put an end to any doubts which still remained with regard to the authenticity of the most hotly disputed entry in the two volumes of the register. Frere had already written the history of Parker's career as archbishop and, as has already been said, had delivered a weighty pronouncement upon its significance in the history of the post-Reformation Church; and his introduction to the first of the three volumes in which the edition was completed was devoted to an analysis of the contents of the whole register and to an explanation of the methods adopted in dealing with the mass of material to avoid unnecessary repetition of common form. As a guide to the procedure of the various departments of archiepiscopal activity represented in the work, this introduction is invaluable. The information with which it is packed abundantly illustrates the continuity of practice in Parker's day with the systems whose origin and development have more recently been traced by Dr. Irene Churchill in her *Canterbury Administration*. While registers of the period are in several instances defective and their contents have to be supplemented from other sources, as in the case of the late C. W.

Foster's edition of *Lincoln Episcopal Records* 1571–1584,
Parker's register is remarkably complete in its comprehensive survey of the necessary business of the province and
diocese and its interest extends far beyond the diocese of
Canterbury. As with the registers of many of his predecessors, the miscellaneous nature of its contents must be kept
in mind, together with the individual responsibility of the
registrar for the selection of his material and for choosing
occasions on which it might conveniently be attended to. If
in these circumstances the searcher does not find everything
that he wants, he will profit at any rate by a method of registration which during the later Middle Ages had greatly
increased in efficiency without developing stereotyped or
narrowly exclusive methods.

The solid contribution which Frere made to the history of
a given period, alike in narrative and in the collection of
documentary illustration, is thus obvious. The position
which he had maintained in *The Marian Reaction* and continued firmly to hold was clearly manifested in a lecture
delivered in 1896 on behalf of the Church Historical Society
and published as one of their tracts with the title, *What is the
Position of the Roman Catholic Body in England?* His gift of
candid and definite statement was excellently employed in
his treatment of the steps by which the alienation of the
English Roman Catholic from the national Church was
accomplished and of the obstacles to reunion at the present
day. At the time he was full of hope that some compromise
might be achieved, and prospects seemed then much brighter
than they became at a later date; but the essential truth of his
position remains the same and cannot be overlooked by the
historian.

Frere's own part in *pourparlers* for reunion is recalled in
his *Recollections of Malines*, published in 1935, his record of
the conferences in which he took part in company with the
late Lord Halifax, Dr. Armitage Robinson and others in
laying the Anglican attitude to reunion before the primate of
Belgium. If these produced no substantial effect, they

formed at any rate an important step in the development of mutual understanding. This, however, is a side of Frere's work which can hardly be treated at length in the present context: necessary as historical knowledge was to any discussions on the subject, their object was one which history could aid but could not decide.

Two works of Frere's, of a very different kind, deserve closing mention. The first, a learned essay on 'The early history of Canons Regular as illustrated by the foundation of Barnwell Priory', appeared in the *Festschrift* presented to the Cambridge antiquary, J. W. Clark, in 1909. Clark himself, whose *Architectural History of the University and Colleges of Cambridge and Eton*, the completion of a work begun by Professor Willis, is one of those works which can never be superseded, had discussed the somewhat difficult and obscure topic of Canons Regular in his *Customs of Augustinian Canons*, an edition of the observances in use at Barnwell with a valuable introduction, and had also edited the *Liber Memorandorum* of the priory at a later period. Frere's essay, with a subject so appropriate to the author as a member of a religious community and to the recipient as one intimately acquainted with its principal theme, does not clear up all the questions raised by consideration of Canons Regular and their peculiar individuality. Some of these still call for satisfactory solution. But the essay called attention to a point that has caused some perplexity to historians of the religious Orders, the original intention of founders of houses of canons to make these monasteries centres of parochial ministrations, shown by the part which gifts of parochial benefices take in their endowments. Of this intention Barnwell is an early example; and although in process of time the practical inconvenience of supplying the cures of souls of appropriated churches by entrusting them to canons became manifest and was checked, the custom survived in certain houses, and in the later Middle Ages considerable latitude was allowed with regard to churches to which the presentation of religious incumbents could be made with some show of reason.

WALTER HOWARD FRERE

Some Links in the Chain of Russian Church History, with a preface dated October 1917, appeared in the following year, at a time when the prospects of the Orthodox Church in Russia were becoming very dark, in spite of the hopes expressed in the preface. Such a book was much needed in view of the growth of sympathy between the English and the Russian Churches and the difference of temperament between the two peoples. No one could have been more fit than Frere to explain the course of Russian Church history to Englishmen. His admiration for the Russian tradition of liturgical worship, his understanding of what cannot but seem to the Western mind the trivial nature of the disputes, unconnected with dogmatic subjects and arising in minute points of ritual practice, which have from time to time split the Orthodox Church into bitterly opposed sections, his personal acquaintance with Russia and the Russian language— all these qualities, used in the service of his overmastering desire for the reunion of the Christian Churches, are clearly visible in his story. As the title shows, it makes no pretence to be a complete history of the Russian Church, but, if its attempt is concentrated upon certain epochs and incidents of special importance, the chain in which they form links is always in sight. The story is told with complete fairness and impartiality by a highly sympathetic observer, and the balanced judgment with which he had regarded the motives and achievements of the English Churchmen of the Reformation period is applied with conspicuous skill, for example, to his estimate of the warring elements in the character of the seventeenth-century patriarch Nikon, or, in more recent times, of the ecclesiastical policy of Pobiedonostsiev during his long tenure of office as Procurator of the Holy Synod. Not the least valuable feature of the book is the select but ample bibliography which precedes it.

If Frere does not take his place among our greatest historians, this is due rather to the specialized nature of the area which he chose for treatment and the limited character of his audience than to any fault of temperament. He set himself to

THE HISTORIAN

his task with clear perception of the ground to be covered; he worked with a firm grip of the subject in hand and a full acquaintance with relevant sources; and there was no ambiguity to be cleared up when his work was done. Under such conditions its authority is permanent: its aim was truth, which ornamental or picturesque writing may distort or obscure, and for its truth, conveyed with an ideal clearness of utterance, it will long be consulted. Further, with all his love and knowledge of the past, Frere never looked backward or played the part of *laudator temporis acti*. To him the Church which he served was no mere relic of times long ago, to be sedulously defended against the dangers and uncertainties of progress: it was a living and growing organism which, in its strife with the temptations of the world, needed contemporary armour. Those who sat with him upon commissions or on the councils of societies to which his advice as historian and antiquary was of the greatest service realized that he was never afraid of testing what to many conservative spirits might seem doubtful novelties and of approving departures which his conscience told him were to the advantage which he sought to procure for his Church. In his aim to 'think clear, feel deeply, bear fruit well' he succeeded, and in that light his historical writings must be judged with no uncertain sentence.

9

THE MUSICIAN

by the late Sir Sydney Nicholson, Dr. J. H. Arnold and Dr. P. A. Browne

Something has already been said in these pages concerning Frere's musical tastes and interests. But music was so fundamental a part of his being, and his own musical achievement so considerable of its kind, that it seems right to dwell more fully on the subject. Nor is material difficult to come by; for Frere had many friends among professional musicians and was never happier than in their company, receiving from them invariably a deference in regard to matters within their own sphere which his modesty would never have dreamed of claiming.

Of these musician friends we are indebted to three for the following contributions, covering various sides of Frere's musical interests and activity.

I

Sir Sydney Nicholson, an intimate friend and for many years closely associated with Frere in connexion with *Hymns Ancient and Modern* and other matters, writes as follows:

'To give a true impression of the part played by music in the life of Walter Frere is a matter of considerable difficulty. His fame as a musician rests mainly on the work he did in connexion with plainchant and hymns. In both these branches his knowledge was profound and the work that he accomplished of the highest importance: indeed in both he was recognized as one of the leading authorities of his time.

'Yet it is true to say that it was not in connexion with the Church that he found his greatest musical enjoyment: indeed it was seldom that actual church music roused him to any real enthusiasm, and with a good deal of it he had little sympathy. The music of the average cathedral service simply bored him: though he held the early composers in respect and would give a hearing to Byrd and Gibbons or even Purcell, their work did not really interest him, while that of most of their successors, with the possible exception of Stanford and Parry, rather annoyed him than otherwise.

'But it was quite another matter with secular music. Almost all orchestral work attracted him; he was a devotee of opera, an enthusiast for songs of the classical type; he rejoiced in Bach and was equally ready to listen to Stravinsky; even the ultra-moderns would receive his full attention, if not his entire approbation.

'It is probably true to say that, outside his ecclesiastical work, music was the greatest interest or "hobby" of his life— but not church music: and it is somewhat ironical that it was in this that he reached the highest distinction, while in the kind of music he most cared for he remained only the amateur, and it cannot even be said that he excelled as a performer when it came to interpreting that which he really loved.

'He had a tenor voice which, as a young man, had been of good quality, and in his singing he certainly "had a way with him", though he could hardly be placed in the first rank. So with his piano-playing: he would dash valiantly at anything set before him, regardless of the number of wrong notes or the vagaries of time: these things did not worry him so long as he felt he could catch the spirit of the music. This was all part of his mental outlook, for with him it was always the music itself that mattered, and the performance of it was comparatively unimportant.

'Yet he thoroughly enjoyed performing. Those who

remember him in early days speak of the constant music-makings during his holidays at Barley Rectory, where there would be much playing by himself on the piano and his brother Arthur on the flute, other members of the family being roped in for frequent part-singing. He seems to have inherited his musical talent from his grandmother, Mrs. Frere (of Downing College, Cambridge), who was an excellent singer, taught by a pupil of Handel, and was described by Edward Fitzgerald as "one of the best judges of music I have known".

'Throughout his life the pleasure in performing remained. Nothing gave him more enjoyment than a turn with two pianos, when he would gaily tackle the most difficult music at sight, not minding in the least the sounds that might result. And at Truro some of his happiest hours were spent with the music club that met weekly at Lis Escop, to sing together.

'Besides choral music of the kind practised at Truro, he had a wide knowledge of opera and orchestral works, aided to some extent by pianola, gramophone and wireless: concert-going and, still more, visits to the opera were always a delight to him, and particularly in Russian music he had a knowledge of many works before they had been heard in England.

'Of his musical compositions not very much need be said, and it is probable that he did not take them very seriously—they were all products of his youth.

'The published works include three albums of songs (bearing no date). There are three Italian songs to words by Jacopo Vittorelli; five songs for baritone, mostly settings of well-known Elizabethan words; and six songs from the *Hesperides* of Robert Herrick. Most of them are comparatively short and simple and have a good melodic line, while the accompaniments are pianistic in treatment. But there is little in the way of thematic development and too often the good start seems to "peter out" before the end.

'The only other published work that seems to exist is of a

later date: "The Order of The Holy Communion set to music in unison for men's voices by the Rev. Walter Howard Frere, Assistant Curate of Stepney Church. Written for the Triennial Festival of the Wells Theological College, 1890, being the fiftieth anniversary of the foundation of the College." (Novello.) This is a curious work, quite unlike what one would expect from its author: e.g. no settings are provided for *Benedictus* and *Agnus Dei*. In style the setting is surprisingly chromatic, and the harmony is often somewhat luscious.

'It is probable that Frere soon realized that his musical gifts did not lie mainly in the direction of composition, and though he seems to have made one or two ventures in connexion with theatrical productions by the students at Mirfield, he published no music in later life.

'Of his contributions to church music as an editor, mention should be made of his best-known work, *The Manual of Plainsong*, in which he collaborated with H. B. Briggs in producing a revised version of the book of the same name issued many years previously by Helmore. This book, familiarly known as "Briggs and Frere", has come to be the most widely used of plainsong psalters.

'But it was in supervising or editing many of the publications of the Plainsong and Medieval Music Society that his most permanently important work was done. He was responsible for the superb facsimile of the Sarum Gradual (1894), and for the three corresponding volumes of the Sarum Antiphoner (1901–24), to each of which he prefixed the deeply learned introduction that only he could write. Another notable piece of research is the *Bibliotheca Musico-Liturgica* (1901, 1932), a list of the medieval musico-liturgical MSS. still surviving in England. His treatment of the device known as "troping" in the introduction to his edition of the *Winchester Troper* (H.B.S., 1894) is classical—and incidentally a most remarkable performance for a young man of thirty. It is not surprising that such work gained for him a European reputation.

'His deep and wide knowledge of plainsong was also shewn in the articles that he contributed to the new edition (1928) of Grove's *Dictionary of Music and Musicians*, edited by his friend and admirer, the late Dr. H. C. Colles. Those on "Plainsong", "Psalmody", "Gregorian Music" and "Mass" are specially extended and important; while he also dealt with such subjects as "Antiphon", "Antiphonal", "Gradual", "Trope" and "Ambrosian Music". In addition he wrote the introductory volume, on 'Plainsong', for *The Oxford History of Music*.

'He was an intimate friend of the Rev. G. H. Palmer, with whom he occasionally collaborated, though in later years he did not altogether see eye to eye with him in the interpretation of plainchant. He was by no means a blind follower of the methods of Solesmes and, indeed, appeared to view many of the *fiats* of that School with a certain amount of suspicion. His own rendering of the chant was certainly not on what have come to be considered in England as orthodox lines: he regarded it and sang it more in the natural style of folk-song than of music guided by strict rules.

'But in this matter, as in many others, it is extremely difficult to formulate what his views were. Never was a man less ready to "lay down the law", at any rate in musical matters; one could only get to understand what he felt by watching his reaction to examples set before him: thus, and thus only, could one gradually come to learn the "sort of thing he liked". But this is far from suggesting that his judgment was based merely on personal preference: if one could ever get at his reasons they were invariably logical and based on deep knowledge. But canons of criticism were rarely forthcoming—he was really too modest in disclosing his learning.

'It may be added that Frere was a member of the Archbishops' Committee on Church Music,[1] which produced a

---

[1] Among Frere's papers survives a lengthy and characteristically eloquent letter from Walford Davies (in bed with the 'flu), expressing mournfully his 'unhappiness' at the perversity of the Committee in various matters and his feeling that 'our greatest danger lies in a conventional association of music with church ritual, ceremonial, traditional use. . . . Music is so much more

valuable report in 1922, outlining an ideal and a policy on the subject that have already issued in important practical results.

'He was closely associated for many years with *Hymns Ancient and Modern*.[1] He was appointed an Assessor in 1894, joined the main body of Proprietors in 1902, and became Chairman in 1923, retaining this post to the end of his life. About the time he joined the committee the lengthy work of revision began which was to result ten years later (1904) in the appearance of the so-called "New Edition". The minute books make it clear that from the outset Frere played a leading part in shaping the new book—in fact, he came to be more and more the life and soul of the whole undertaking. His expert knowledge of music was of special value; and he acted as the link between the committee and the distinguished musicians whose co-operation was enlisted. An entry dated 9th Jan. 1896 records that "Mr. Frere was requested to invite the following gentlemen to serve on the music committee, and to preside over them as Chairman—Dr. Stanford, Sir Walter Parratt, H. E. Wooldridge, B. Luard Selby, Charles Wood and Dr. Steggall *ex officio*." He himself, in the

than an acolyte, a stole, or even a whole ceremonial.' Frere, in reply, suggests that not all can express their penitence or worship in song. 'Let the musician sing his homage by all means, but most people will express theirs by genuflecting, or bowing, or something of the sort; indeed, personally, I always feel that I come nearer expressing the homage in the silence of a gesture than one can in words or in music even when unfettered by words. That is what I feel we are after. Is it really so wicked as you say?' To which Walford Davies replies enthusiastically, 'How lovely to receive your letter: and let me say how precious your friendship is to me.'

[1] A permanent memorial of this exists concerning which Canon Lowther Clarke, D.D., furnishes the following note:

'The Proprietors of *Hymns Ancient and Modern*, whose practice it is to use their profits in making donations to charities, in the course of a number of years made substantial grants to the Society for the Promotion of Christian Knowledge. The Society kept the money intact, and some years after the Bishop's death offered to use it and the accrued interest to form a 'Walter Howard Frere Fund', the interest on which should be available for various objects in connexion with hymnody and church music, and primarily the publication of works of research in the field of hymnody. The offer was gratefully accepted by the Community of the Resurrection, and also commended itself to the Proprietors'.

matter of both words and tunes, brought to light many fine things that had been forgotten or were practically unknown.

'Owing to a variety of causes, some of them most trivial, the book was a failure. A violent press campaign—"Hands off our old Favourites!"—raised a storm of protest, and prejudice was aroused amongst many who had never actually seen the book itself. Perhaps the greatest outcry was raised by the restoration of the original opening of Wesley's Christmas hymn, to "Hark how all the welkin rings". The result was that the book was doomed almost before publication.

'Nevertheless it was undoubtedly the finest and most representative collection that had so far appeared. On the heels of this *débâcle* other new books soon made their appearance, and hymns, and especially tunes, that had been brought to light in the 1904 book were "rediscovered" and hailed with enthusiasm as wonderful finds: for prejudice had by this time died down, and a completely new book had a chance of being considered on its merits now that the 1904 book had paved the way.

'But if the 1904 book failed in its popular appeal it had at least one permanent result in the *Historical Edition of Hymns Ancient and Modern*, which appeared in 1909. Though Frere was practically entirely responsible for this huge piece of work it is characteristic of him that his name appears but once in its pages—and not on the title page! Yet it is his most important contribution to the study of church music and is generally regarded as the standard book on the subject. Incidentally, it was accepted by Cambridge University as its author's thesis for the D.D. degree.

'A large volume of some thousand pages, it begins with a hundred-page Introduction, which deals with the whole question of hymns and tunes and their origins, enriched with many illustrations and facsimiles. This part of the book alone is a monument of scholarship. The last section of the Introduction gives an interesting account of the origins and development of *Hymns A. and M.* and the genesis of the 1904 revision.

'The main section of the Historical Edition consists of the text of all the 643 hymns and tunes contained in the 1904 book together with certain other tunes included in the old edition but not the new. Besides the English words the original of all Latin and Greek hymns is given in full, and below each hymn are full notes as to origins of both words and music, original versions of tunes being added in all cases where variants have arisen. To the student these notes are simply invaluable, and the labour of collecting and arranging such a mass of information must have been prodigious.

'The book is completed with a wonderful series of Indices, including biographical notes of authors and composers, and a chronological list of tunes. The compilation of indices amounted almost to a hobby with the author; his wonderfully accurate mind seemed to rejoice in a task which to most people is no more than complicated drudgery.

'In this connexion is perhaps the best place to add a personal note by one who had the privilege of acting under him as Musical Editor for a period of some twenty-five years, and seeing through the press under his guidance the Second Supplement of 1916, merged later in the Standard Edition, the *Plainsong Hymnbook*, 1932, and the Shortened Music Edition completed just before his death and published in 1939.

'Frere's methods were peculiar. Most of his directions and suggestions and pieces of information were written in the tiniest handwriting on post-cards or small scraps of paper, with copious use of abbreviations, so that one small card might contain information on dozens of different matters. Many of these missives were at first difficult to interpret and somewhat bewildering: but in time the technique was grasped, for the writing though microscopic was marvellously clear and details were invariably accurate.

'On his many journeys to the Continent and to various libraries it was his custom to carry small note-books, sometimes with ruled music lines, but more often plain with the lines drawn as required; in these he would note down tunes with their sources as he came across them. A good many were "modern" tunes, but the majority were medieval or plainsong, and it was from the latter that much of the material for the *Plainsong Hymnbook* was garnered. This book, the contents of which were decided almost entirely by Frere himself, was only made possible by his wide collection of material, and it contains many beautiful tunes that are not to be found elsewhere. There can be little doubt that he was more personally interested in this book than in any of the other hymnals with which he was associated, and though it is greatly to be regretted that it has never come into general use it remains, like the Historical Edition, a monument of his learning.

'As to his personal taste in hymn-tunes, it is true to say that those he really cared for were almost entirely the plainsong melodies. But he had a good critical appreciation of "modern" tunes and would not hesitate to condemn an old Psalm-tune if he thought it dull, or to accept a Victorian specimen if he thought it good of its kind: he had not very much use for the eighteenth-century tunes (such as "Richmond") which formed such a feature of later books, even though he had included a good many of the best of them in the 1904 book. Certain things he abominated: Welsh hymn-tunes, late French "cookings" of plainsong, particularly those in Sapphic metre, like the Rouen Church melodies; and—Merbecke! It is curious that he had not a good word to say for this famous work; to him it was simply plainsong spoiled, and that was all there was about it; even the parts that had clearly nothing to do with plainsong he brushed aside as poor stuff. He was by no means highbrow in his taste, though he did not always realize that what to him might be attractive would very likely not appeal to an ordinary congregation. This may account for the large number of tunes of German origin which appeared in 1904— fine things in themselves, but hardly of the style that English churchgoers readily assimilate. But he was often frankly philistine, and he enjoyed his Dykes and Stainer as well as his Bach and Gibbons.

'It would not be right to conclude this sketch of his musical life without mentioning Frere's extraordinary modesty in musical matters. Though he held strong opinions he would mention them only with diffidence, and a casual acquaintance would be led to think that his knowledge of the subject was no more than that of the enthusiastic amateur. But the same quality applied to his other interests which were many and diverse, so that in conversing on almost any subject his partner would only gradually come to realize that here was a man who probably knew far more about it than himself.

'Perhaps it was on the musical side that he was most unbending or, one might almost say, most cheerful. Anything to do with music, even hymns which (it must be confessed) sometimes bored him, seemed to bring him into a happy frame of mind, so that all who worked with him in this field will remember him less as the learned theologian, the ascetic monk, or the much-tried bishop, than as the joyous companion and the unique friend.'

2

Another friend, Dr. J. H. Arnold, contributes the following, dealing particularly with Frere's work on behalf of plainsong:

'My first sight of Dr. Frere was in Westminster Abbey when on some weekday evening the lean agile monkish figure walked swiftly through the choir up to those brass rails—now happily gone—that fenced the sacrarium. He was one of the early apostles of the truly congregational singing of Creed, Sanctus and Gloria in the Eucharist, and he had come to teach us, as so well he could, to take our part in singing Merbecke. Is it necessary to say that he soon had us singing the old music, swiftly and pliantly, as though it had always been ours?

'My next contact was on the unforgettable occasion when, at an Alcuin Club meeting in the Westbourne Terrace

Priory, he first read his paper on the Primitive Consecration Prayer, since published by the Club. Then I beheld that almost wizardly power of his not only to unravel a tangled skein before our eyes, but to hold it up as it were as a glittering crystal ball, clear and limpid, which he seemed dexterously to toss in his lean fingers. It remains, I believe, a masterpiece.

'One meeting remains specially vivid. It was my birthday, I think, and Miss Eleanor Gregory had invited my wife and me to lunch with her in her beautiful house at Whitchurch near Aylesbury—Mary Monk's Close. I needed no lure, but she had promised me a birthday surprise. It was revealed as we sat after lunch in the faery rose-scented tall-hedged garden, when down the long grass path came the familiar lean black figure of her "dear Walter", not quite so agile (for he had been ill), but with eyes atwinkle and voice as musical and buoyant as ever. He was himself, though I noticed his tiredness after the walk to which he had so readily assented after tea.

'We walked and talked, I remember, much to my profit of course, of the facsimile Sarum Processional I had undertaken to edit for the Plainsong Society. How well I remember his hard words for the "Antiscrape" in their treatment of a church—was it Whitchurch?—into which we turned. But I thought he placed the blame for its coldness on the wrong shoulders; to me the "Antiscrape" had laid good foundations for a liturgical architect. I admit I was never able to have the complete trust in his taste that I had in his scholarship and judgment elsewhere, and I think he exposed a weak side in some of his translations for the *Plainsong Hymnbook* (*A. and M.*). But then, he never liked the sequences: he thought them dull, though I wrung from him the confession that he would except the Advent *Salus aeterna* (E.H. 10) and the Rosy Sequence (E.H. 238). Yet, in his translations, he never wavered from the inner rhythm of the music; and was it not for musical reasons that he saw to the punctuation of the Proper Prefaces in the 1928 rite? And indeed was not the

Canon of that rite his work? It exactly expresses his judgment.

'Meetings of the Council of the Plainsong Society were always enlivened by his presence—his smile, his sparkle, his humour, his shrewd business sense; but above all, his profound knowledge which sat so lightly on him, and was always at anybody's disposal.

'And who was as easy of approach? Well I remember, in the chapel of the S.E.C.M. at Chislehurst, begging him to tell me the provenance of an old Antiphoner which lay there open on a desk. Instantly he was fingering the pages, and almost as swiftly the date of the book was known. Was the feast of St. Francis there? And many other things he told me of it. It was a pretty sight to see his ascetic fingers play in an old manuscript.

'Surely one encounters such rare spirits but once on an earthly pilgrimage.'

3

On no occasion was Frere's very individual reaction to music and music-making more clearly revealed than at his Tuesday gatherings for choral singing at Lis Escop. Of these Dr. P. A. Browne, one of H.M. Inspectors, furnishes the following sketch:

'Others can tell of the beginnings of the singing meetings at Lis Escop. When I came to Cornwall in 1931 they were in full swing. Anything from eight to twenty men and women came up about three times a month, according to the Bishop's engagements; we sat round the table in the dining-room and sang from eight till about a quarter-past ten, with an interval for coffee and biscuits. Bach Cantatas had pride of place before the interval; they were usually selected so as to be appropriate to the season, though occasionally the choice was dictated, in something like the way Bach's own choices were dictated, by the forces at the Bishop's disposal on a particular night. Afterwards we usually tackled something more modern. The Bishop's taste was catholic and his repertoire was quite wide; I never asked him, but I strongly suspect that it was built up rather at random from Mr. Harold Reeves's catalogue of "Second-hand vocal scores in quantities". There was a good deal of Brahms, Parry, Stanford and Vaughan Williams, some Russian Church Music, Holst's "Ode to Death", Humperdinck's "Voyage to Kevlaar", Walford Davies's "Everyman", Purcell's "Te Deum in D", Bainton's "Sunset at Sea", Schumann's "Advent Hymn", to mention a few works at random. There were surprising gaps; Handel was represented by "Israel in Egypt" alone, and that we did but once while I was there; of Mendelssohn there were two psalms only; there was nothing of Haydn's, Mozart's or Beethoven's.

'Conditions were not easy: the room was large, the piano not only a bit "woolly" but rather far from the singers, so that it was difficult while singing to feel the support we might have expected from the "orchestra". Moreover, although there was no doubt that as we went on we improved very substantially in sight reading, we were by no means a picked body of trained musicians, and many of us were overawed and rendered self-conscious, to a greater extent than it probably ever occurred to him to guess, by the Bishop's own presence and personality. At the same time, we were never deterred from tackling a work on mere grounds of difficulty; performances of the "Sea Symphony" or the "Dream of Gerontius" were as frequent as those of "Phaudrig Crohoore" or the "Death of Minnehaha". One natural consequence was that courage and enthusiasm had to take the place of accuracy and finish, and the occasional visitors who came to listen to our efforts must have been singularly sympathetic, complaisant, or insensitive, if they came a second time. The Bishop's interest lay in the music and not in the rendering; often he would comment at the end of a dreadfully uneven performance, "Wasn't that splendid?" His attitude rather reminded me of César Franck's; and I should not be surprised if for his musical meetings he adopted the motto: "If a thing's worth doing at all it is worth doing badly."

'All the same, we enjoyed the meetings tremendously, and I believe he did; we made the acquaintance of much fine music that we should never otherwise have met, at any rate at such close quarters; we had the pleasure of singing and reading; and above all we had the privilege of finding ourselves in the company of a great man in his hours of relaxation. None of us is likely to forget various small personal touches and actions of the Bishop's; as I think back over those meetings at Lis Escop I have a vivid memory of him kneeling at the low cupboards in which the music was stored searching for some elusive work that he was determined to unearth, or pointing a friendly but admonitory finger at some unlucky contralto who had missed her lead, or giving the lead himself in a dominating falsetto. My chief recollection of his actual performances is of the breathy, half-whispered crotchet on the word "Death" at the end of the first chorus of Stanford's "Elegiac Ode", where the rest of the parts hold out calmly for two whole bars. Then I think of the "Sanctus, Fortis" in the "Dream of Gerontius", in which he would exhibit a musical understanding and a fervour that triumphed over the frailties of age and tiredness. For his voice still had a beautiful quality, though it was already old and tired when I first met him.

'A society that meets for reading through choral works, with no thought of public performance and with not only no emphasis on, but even with a tradition against, going over numbers and passages that have gone wrong with a view to putting them right, where the music is everything and the standard of performance nothing, may not be unique, but it is very rare, and in my opinion it is the best kind of choral society. I think our principles rather offended some of our distinguished visitors, but they suited the Bishop and they suited us, and we went gaily on our way.

'Apart from the choral meetings I had the privilege of being occasionally invited up to Lis Escop for a musical evening. Sometimes we would listen to some broadcast work—characteristically the Bishop's set did not always afford very good reception—and sometimes he would sing Parry, Stanford, Wolf, or Russian songs; occasionally we would play duets—Borodin's 1st Symphony or Moskowski's Spanish Dances. I remember that he pointed out to me that the Parry songs that are usually sung in public are by no means the best, and he introduced me to a whole range of his most impressive quiet and reflective songs. If I had not known better, I think I should have come away from these evenings with the opinion that the Bishop's musical interest lay solely with the Russians, the moderns, and the late nineteenth-century English composers. This is only one example of the way in which his wholehearted enthusiasm for whatever he was engaged on at the moment could momentarily obscure one's recognition of his encyclopædic knowledge and the vast range of his interests. In much the same way, he was one of those people who are able to give you the impression that you are the one person they have been hoping the whole evening to get the chance of a word with. . . .

'My abiding recollection is of a great man who influenced for good all who came in contact with him. I remember with gratitude his charm, his cheerfulness, his courtesy, his humour; I respectfully admired the attainments of a scholar who never intruded his scholarship; but I suppose that the central quality that made him so impressive a figure was his saintliness—a positive and active saintliness that illuminated his every word and action, and combined with the maximum consideration for others an inflexible will and an almost terrifying singleness of purpose.'

4

Finally, by way of appendix, it may be interesting to print a letter by Frere himself, written to his friend Hugh Stewart in answer to a query of Bishop John Wordsworth of Salisbury as to what to say in dedicating an organ. It illustrates his ready and recondite learning, and culminates in an amusing tirade against organs and organists.

THE MUSICIAN

Trin. Coll. Oxon., Sept 11 '00.

I fancy instrumental music was not used [in the early centuries of the Christian Church] because it wasn't good enough. Lutes were the only things much available for accompaniment, and I fancy that lute-playing was gone and done with in Greco-Roman circles by the third century. The existing Cantilena Romana was originally in the lute modes of this Greco-Roman period and was elaborate with the sort of elaboration and embroidery which is characteristic of unaccompanied singing. The *fioriture* are the making of unaccompanied melodies.

But, of course, as you know, the earlier methods before St. Augustine and St. Ambrose were simpler. Responsorial psalmody was all that there was in the West till then, and it was *pronuncianti vicinior quam canenti*. Responsorial psalmody could not be congregational in any other way. It was mere inflected monotone with a short refrain. When St. Ambrose brought in the antiphonal method *tunes* began to appear, and so too with his hymns melody began to come in. And then very soon the elaborate chant both antiphonal and responsorial which St. Gregory pruned and stamped with his genius.

I suppose there was a bit of Puritan spirit in it too. In the first three centuries there was the horror of what smacked of the theatre: and when that began to fade instrumental music was fading too. When it revived it soon attacked the plain chant of the church: organs were at first happily rare: they never can have done anything but spoil the music—as they do still. I wish the bishops would from the point of view of church music do anything but bless organs. These great bellowing things which every twopenny organist now wants to run riot on spoil the singing and rob the congregation of their rights and duties, besides disfiguring the churches and prolonging the services far beyond the time which the average laity are prepared gladly to give. Every little parish church apes the worst faults of cathedrals till one can't wonder that the folk fly in despair to the *banalité* of the Chapel instead, as a more tolerable infliction.

173

After all, a surpliced choir is not an article of the Christian Faith. And the congregation has more right to be considered than an organist. I hope the Bishop will lift up his parable against musical excesses. . . . They do far more harm and alienate more people than ceremonial excesses do.

That is what I should like to say at the dedication of an organ! . . .

I am in retreat at the pseudo-Trin. Coll. and must to bed now.

10

SPIRITUAL LIFE AND INFLUENCE

by the late Evelyn Underhill and C. S. Phillips

T he biographer of Walter Frere can hardly avoid being haunted by an uncomfortable feeling that he is doing something which Frere himself would have regarded with very slight enthusiasm. Most of all would he have hated any attempt to lift the veil from his inner life. Here at least, however, there is not even the temptation to offend; for the requisite materials simply do not exist.

Many of the most famous exponents of Christian sanctity seem to have found little difficulty in exposing the secret places of their hearts to the gaze of others—and no doubt posterity has every reason to be grateful for the unreserve of an Augustine and a Teresa. But for Frere such things were his own affair and no one else's. He never talked about them even to his most intimate friends, and could hardly help wincing when others were less reticent about themselves. Still less did he expatiate on them in his letters. Only in his interleaved copy of Bishop Andrewes's *Devotions* and in a few prayers that he wrote for others can we still catch the particular quality of his piety. A specimen of each kind (in Latin and English respectively), one belonging to his earlier, the other to his later years, will be found in a note at the end of this chapter.

Of course, the spiritual quality of the man could not but be seen shining through its physical envelope, which indeed always seemed to be an illustration of the famous line, 'For soul is form and doth the body make'—an illustration displaying itself not only in face and figure but in voice and manner as well. Even those who disliked Frere's views and rejected his leadership were often quite ready to admit that he was 'a saint'. In him, in fact, was seen in an altogether exceptional degree that quality of the Supernatural which was a favourite theme of one of the greatest and deepest of modern religious thinkers, the late Baron Friedrich von Hügel. We may make the assertion the more confidently because von Hügel himself noted this quality in Frere in the comment already quoted at the head of chapter 5. The idea of the Supernatural is not perhaps very familiar to the generality of thoughtful people nowadays; and those who wish to understand it must study it in von Hügel's own writings.[1] But the following brief quotation may help to explain it and to suggest the quality in Frere which struck von Hügel and so many others:

'We have to discriminate not simply between Evil and Good, but between Good and Good, between Natural Good and Supernatural Good. . . . The morality of honest barter, of moderate living; the requirements of the counting-house, the law-courts, the State; Confucius, Bentham; such moralities, institutions, persons . . . are assuredly good and necessary, but they are natural . . . they do not of themselves suggest or require the heightened consciousness, the closer and closest intercourse with God, the reaching, in Him, of the ultimate Living Beauty, Truth and Goodness, which the religious soul seeks when it seeks Immortal Life. . . . All such heroic, self-oblivious search and receipt of Truth and Beauty, as possessing the right to such self-surrender, appear a special divine gift rather than mere human effort, as glimpses of realities which, for their adequate environment and apprehension, require not this world and this life, but another life and another world.'

[1] See e.g. *Essays and Addresses on the Philosophy of Religion.* pp. 198–200 (from which the quoted extract is taken), also the remarkable discourse on 'Christianity and the Supernatural,' *ib.* 278–98.

__32,4.__ 1 Compact made daily   My initiative yes in a sense.
                                  But God is originator : teach.
            I will a bold venture = reckless as a human bargain.
                                      justifiable as one w^t God.
        This reciprocity is base of all : & halves. He to me. / to Him.
2. first promise "to the end".   each indispensable.
    (a) How long since [profess?] [what persevere
                                  [what relapses drop things.
    (b) progressive standard 'not keep' a fixed level.
        "   ∴ God teaches ∴ 'to the end' & more required.
3. Second promise whole heart i.e. not duration but intensity.
        harder test. E.g we do keep prayers offices but intensity
            so too keeping of. discipline.
            [Silence. wholehearted: Negative: or intelligent?
            [Obedience   "   halfhearted: or reluctant?
    ∴ Recover the mutual bargain.
    Renew the two points of promise.

__35,6.__ Reflection I cant go ∴ make me to go. I cant be wholehearted ∴ [make me such].
            Otherwise we are in Pelagianism.
                    think sin is only lack of knowledge   Teach & I will
                        pardonable in Socrates: not Xⁿ nor even human.
i Fallacy of self-confidence.
    (a) Theory fails. Man not selfsufficient.
                      has Will as mainspring: but must be wound up.
        + in his surroundings is no perpetual motion.
            only in God is source of all motion.
    (b) Practice fails   So usual cause of failure.
                          Is there any other?

2. Causes of self-confidence
    (a) obstinacy   I won't be 'made'   You needn't. God wont force
                                          but you fail
                    if doubtful as regards relⁿ to God: test elsewhere. E.g. City.
    (b) pride.   I wont be helped.   Not say so in theory but act so.
                    we say Teach me but think we know
                              Act teach settle for ourselves
3. For want of surrender + humility. we fail.
        We want good: but it is 'covetousness' not desire.
                    i.e wanting things wh: we have no [right to .]
                                                  [for.]
        when we surrender: then 'desire'
                    i.e want + be willing to do what is needed to get:
    Magnify this desire Religⁿ is a scheme for [kindling] and desire
                                                        [enlarging]
            [like worlds] then desire are th[ ][ ] satisfied.

Thus with Frere one was ever aware of the *differentia* of the Christian Life, as contrasted with other modes of living. And, this being so, it was inevitable that his spiritual outlook and experience should breathe through his sermons and addresses, for all their studied reticence and restraint. Dr. Rendall bears striking witness to this: 'I recall', he writes, 'an Ascension Day sermon at Winchester which left the school gasping, as through some Beatrice had led them for a little while up the golden stairs. He made spiritual mysteries seem real and accessible even to schoolboys. He had in fact the gift of infectious spirituality.'

Specially noteworthy is the last sermon that he preached before the University of Cambridge (on 13th October 1935), in which—expanding the thought, *Vocatus iterum atque iterum*, already set down in his Bishop Andrewes forty years before—he seemed to look back on and to sum up the 'Divine encounters' of a lifetime. Based on the striking text, 'I turned to see the voice . . . and being turned, I saw' (Rev. i. 12), the sermon opens thus:

'So began the Revelation entrusted to St. John in Patmos. With a right about turn. And being turned he saw; and all the rest followed.'

It then goes on to illustrate the various ways in which man 'turns' to God. In childhood, at school, 'of all stages of life the one least adapted for dramatic turns'. Then:

'The next stage is very different. The school religion may easily scale off on leaving; but the moment is at hand for a fresh trumpet-call, a fresh turn and fresh vision. Freed from the team, and without the encouragement and the restrictions of school life, the undergraduate can or must again take his own line, and he is called upon to make all the past religious experience his own by his own fresh personal profession of allegiance to our Lord Christ.

'Cambridge knows very well from its own history how rich this opportunity can be: and how it can ripen into various forms of expression. Men and women have found here their Saviour in their undergraduate days. We know it

and thank God for it generation after generation. They have
heard here their call to turn and see. They have turned and
seen afresh the old Hero of their childish days; they have
fallen at His feet with an enlarged loyalty; and seen Him,
not merely as the Hero whom they feel bound to copy, but
also as the Master whom they pledge themselves to serve.
The forms which religious conversion takes—like the circumstances which lead up to it—vary infinitely. They exhibit
all the rich diversity of God's ways with His children. But
all comes back to the simple phrases, "I turned and saw:
and I fell at His feet". . . .

'When does this opportunity end? Never while life lasts.
The call may sound louder though the outward ears may
have gone deaf. The failing eyesight may see better than ever
before. The poor body may be paralysed and unable to turn;
but not so the soul. . . . The trumpet still sounds: the turning
is still possible: the vision has not faded: nor shall the renewal
of our homage cease. . . . So there is call, turn, and vision for
all of us right up to the end.'

What was true of his preaching was true also of his dealings with individual souls. Here too he never failed to give
from the stores of his own knowledge of the things of eternity
to those who sought his help and guidance. No one could
approach him thus without realizing his profound spirituality, just as those to whom he ministered in suffering of
body or mind can never forget the sympathy and unstinting
helpfulness which yet had nothing of softness about them,
but seemed to challenge the sufferer to climb at least as near
the heroic level as it was in him to do. Yet he never *sought*
confidences—he had nothing of the urge to penetrate the
secrets of others and to assume responsibility for their lives
which has marked many great religious leaders. He had an
unfailing respect for personality. In the same way he never
'improved the occasion' by edifying discourse. For him religion was all in all; but he wanted to live it, not talk about it.
So again when in his last years he had to suffer a good deal
(far more than he allowed others to realize) he never spoke

either of his trials or of the 'interior consolations' which helped him to put up with them.

All this may seem very negative and unsatisfying to those who like to probe the secrets of the saintly character. But in the case of Walter Frere we have got to be content with the result: the process and method by which it was achieved are hidden from our eyes. Something a little more positive, however, may perhaps be gleaned from what Fr. Talbot has said in his chapter on Frere's life at Mirfield, and from the following 'memories' which the late Evelyn Underhill, an intimate friend and one of his 'penitents', wrote for this memoir some time before her death:

'Baron von Hügel used to say of Bishop Frere that he "looked like the eagle come off the lectern", but added that nothing—not even a bishopric—could spoil his simplicity, naturalness and humility. This double impression is what first comes to mind when one thinks of him—that almost medieval aristocratic or ecclesiastical transcendency of a scholar and churchman, combined with a great simplicity, limitless interest in and loving consideration for his fellow-creatures, and delight in the detail of life. He loved all the types and oddities of human nature; and by no means cared for the ultra pious most. In fact, I think he found particular refreshment in the natural goodness of the unchurched soul. He was full of fun, and had a certain dancing gaiety which made one instinctively associate him with the ideas of music and light, and which ill-health and overwork never wholly expelled. "How are you?" said an old friend towards the close of his life. "Like the Cheshire Cat, slowly fading away," answered the Bishop, and one could well believe that his smile would be the last thing left.

'The fact that he had been formed by a monastic discipline, though it never intruded on the social side of life, could still be felt as a controlling factor in all his relationships. In fact, perhaps his most marked characteristic was the perfect harmony between an extreme but hidden personal austerity, a ceaseless and literal application of the Evangelical Counsels to the details of his own life, with a great aesthetic sensibility. There was no conflict here. The intense feeling for perfection in music, words, painting—in fact, in our whole use of things—which would tolerate nothing slovenly or second-rate either in sacred or secular life, and regarded bad and careless handwriting as an offence against God, was a true part of his religion; which made the whole of life, at every level, the material of worship and self-offering. The care and neatness with which his notes or music were kept, the stern criticism of those who tried to "get away" with a sloppy sentence or ambiguous phrase, the quiet and delicate love with which he tended his chapel at Lis Escop—all these were various expressions of his profound incarnationalism; his sense of man's responsibility to God in respect of his use of things.

'Like all great Christians, he was a realist—but Christian realism has many forms of expression. For Father Frere I think that his religion was above all a personal relationship; it seemed indeed to have little or no metaphysical side, and I am sure that he would never have agreed with von Hügel's definition of it as a "metaphysical thirst". His strong historical feeling and sense of the continuity of religion did to some extent affect the form in which his spirituality was expressed. His devotion seemed to demand embodiment, and sought it by preference in liturgic and historical forms. Hence his love of the past, his delight in the ancient Christian relics of Cornwall, and attempts to restore an interest in its saints and pilgrimages to their shrines. At confirmations he introduced the taking of a saint's name by each child confirmed; but the last time I asked him how this had prospered he answered that it only survived in one (very extreme and troublesome) parish "where all the girls are called Joseph and all the boys are called Mary".

'Connected with this sense of historical continuity was his great concern for liturgy, and for form and order in the devotional life. But here, too, his realistic temper constantly intervened to check excesses with a reminder of the reason

for all that was done. The regular saying of the Divine Office
—though "I often cut Compline in the holidays"—was a
way of adoring communion with God; perhaps more precious
and less open to distraction when said alone than in choir. It
"began with a hermit and a Bible". Early Mass with communion, and Evensong, were "a very Christian way of spending Sunday". As to High Mass, for himself he found it very
difficult to "do the same thing twice". He disliked the practice of hearing Mass without communicating; and thought it
an unwholesome deformation of the liturgy. *Sursum Corda*
shows what importance he attached to routine intercessions;
and how much less, in comparison, was his sympathy with
formless prayer. He used to tell—a bit against himself—the
story of a discussion on prayer at the Anglo-Russian Conference at High Leigh which was opened by a Cuddesdon
student with an account of his own methodical devotions:
carefully prepared daily meditations, special intercessions and
thanksgivings for each day of the week. "I was just thinking,"
said the Bishop, "how nice all this is! How *very* nice!" when
a Russian girl exclaimed in a voice of horror: 'But I thought
we were going to discuss *Prayer*.' "

'Nevertheless the adoring temper of Russian spirituality
appealed to him profoundly; and I suspect, its austere side
too—for though on the surface so easy, genial and unrigor-
ous, an occasional phrase would reveal the iron foundations
on which his inner life was really built. "I regard sitting on
the least comfortable chair as *very* important," he said suddenly, when someone mentioned a priest who had recommended this exercise to his penitents; and on another occasion when discussing solemn vows, he exclaimed, "Why
worry with vows when one has given one's whole life?" and
then shut up abruptly, as if afraid that he had said too much.

'What those who railed at him as a "monk" did not always
realize was that, had he not been a Catholic, Bishop Frere
would have been a fervent Evangelical of the best type.
Behind all his love of beauty, order and tradition was the
intimate personal link. It was appropriate that during his

WALTER HOWARD FRERE

episcopate the altar in memory of Henry Martyn was set up in the cathedral—for there was a certain likeness in the realistic Christocentricism of these two scholar-saints. To be with Bishop Frere in a church where the Blessed Sacrament was reserved was to feel that he was, in a special sense, in the presence of an intimate Friend; and there was a peculiar and touching beauty in his gesture of farewell on the threshold as he came away. Though in the technical sense he could not be called a mystic, he certainly lived in the presence of the Invisible and in constant and dutiful dependence upon the action of God.

'In his method of directing souls there was nothing very new or startling; but here again an unrelenting realism as regards the relation of the soul to God. He taught in the great central tradition of Christian spirituality, and certainly set a high value on method and order—regular meditation, examen, routine intercessions, etc. But even here he was never rigid, and always keenly aware of the difference in souls. The combined common sense, actuality and spirituality so characteristic of St. François de Sales, was prominent in his teaching. It was not, however, always easy to get definite advice or opinions from him, for his humility always made him diffident and tentative in his approach to other souls. But if there was a real "spot of trouble" demanding help and care, he sprang to attention at once without any consideration for his own convenience or arrangements, like a skilful surgeon confronted by a case for immediate operation. Then he spoke and advised firmly and with an absolute certainty, going straight to fundamentals and cutting out all merely personal considerations, and transforming the situation by his touch. Subsequent thanks for help rendered would probably be acknowledged by a postcard, "Laus Deo!"—the two words which more than any others summed up the intention of his inner and his outer life.'

NOTES

I

de Ev. S. Joannis
Sept. '99

IESU CHRISTE FILI DEI UIUI

Agnus Dei	mitem me fac
Pastor bone	fac strenuum et fidelem
Per exemplum tuum	da tua imitari
Hospes in Cana	laetantibus congaudere, laetitiam augere
Instructor Nicodemi	quaerentibus uacare et praesertim timidis
Correptor Samaritanae	inconuictos conuincere, eciam in uia
Sanator filii Nobilis	anxiatos consolari
Saluator aegri in Bethesda	aegrotantibus subuenire
Miserator in turbas	esurientes implere
Laborantibus et perterritis tutamen	labores metusque mitigare
Decidentibus sustentamen	de imbecillis non desperare
Adulterae moriturae tegmen	conuictis parcere et misereri
Caeci medicamen et etiam solamen	persecutis propter iusticiam astare
Amicus familiae in Bethania	amicis et cognatis non deesse
Mariae bonis operis uindicator	benefactorum non obliuisci
Humilis in pedilauio	da humilitatem erga fratres et subditos
Mansuetus in buccella	da misericordiam erga inimicos
Anxius de Simone	da sollicitudinem erga periclitantes
Prouidus de deserentibus	da curam erga contristantes
Tener in Malchum	da magnanimitatem erga oppugnantes
Tacitus sub conuiciis	da silencium coram malignantibus
Immotus sub tormentis	da paciencium coram cruciantibus
Memor aliorum eciam in morte	da caritatem sui obliuiscentem
Moriens in cruce	da mortificacionem sibi non parcentem
Magdalenae consolator	lugentibus fac solacium
Apostolorum corroborator	titubantibus fac subsidium
Thomae persuasor	dubitantibus fac praesidium
Piscatorum refeccio	deficientibus fac auxilium
Simonis restaurator	poenitentibus fac remedium.

+

2

SUSPIRIA ANIME
UIX AMANTIS DEUM

A FRATRE SCRIPTA

A SORORIBUS IMPRESSA

IN PRELO CONUENTUS BEATE MARIE VIRGINIS

WANTAGE

A.S. MCMXX.

+

WALTER HOWARD FRERE

LOVE

My God, I desire to love Thee perfectly:
With all my heart which Thou
madest for Thyself,
With all my mind which only Thou canst satisfy,
With all my soul which fain would soar to Thee,
With all my strength, my feeble strength,
which shrinks before so great a task,
and yet can choose nought else but spend itself in loving Thee.
Claim Thou my heart, Fill Thou my mind,
Uplift my soul, and Reinforce my strength,
That where I fail Thou mayest succeed in me,
and make me love Thee perfectly.

+

FEAR

I fear Thee, O my God.
O righteous Father,
with a filial awe,
O Judge inexorable, with guilty dread,
O Holy Ghost, with terror born of sacrilege.
I fear Thee, O my God:
And fearing Thee I fear naught else;
Not life, nor death, nor hell,
Not man, nor fiend,
But only Thee,
My God.

+

PATIENCE

My God I can wait   If Thou uphold me:
I can endure   If Thou sustain me:
I can give up   If Thou reward me:
I gladly will do all   If Thou command me:
O righteous Judge, Thou art both strong and patient,
I will be patient if Thou make me strong.

+

DESIRE

Lord, I desire, I desire,
I cannot say how much:
I only know I stand in need of all things.
And would that my desire were as great as is my need!
Lord, who alone canst satisfy the human heart's desire,
And fill with all Thy fulness the abyss of human need,
Hear now how I desire all good things,
And Thee, Thyself, my God, above all else,
Who givest all.

+

11

BISHOP FRERE AND THE RUSSIAN ORTHODOX CHURCH

by Dr. Nicolas Zernov

There were two periods in Bishop Frere's life in which he came into close fellowship with the Russian Christians, and each of these forms an important page in his biography as well as in the history of Anglican-Orthodox relations.

His early contacts with the Russian Church took place in the years immediately preceding the outbreak of the first World War. Walter Frere paid at that time three visits to Russia. He went there first with his sister in May-June 1909, when, as representative of Cambridge University, he attended the celebrations in commemoration of the Russian writer Nicholas Gogol (1809–52) at the unveiling of his monument in Moscow. In August 1910 Walter Frere again spent a month in Russia, mostly in Finland and the Baltic Provinces. This time it was purely a holiday trip. His last and most important visit took place in the winter of 1914. He was away from England from January till March, and in the course of these months he delivered a number of addresses in Riga, Polotsk, St. Petersburg, Moscow, and in the Monastery of the Holy Trinity founded by St. Sergius of Radonezh.

This lecture tour was organized by the Russian Society for promoting *rapprochement* between the Anglican and Eastern Orthodox Churches. This new organization was founded in 1912[1] as a parallel body to the Anglican and Eastern Orthodox Church Union started in England in 1906 by a group of keen enthusiasts for Christian Reunion —a group which included Revs. H. J. Fynes Clinton, J. A. Douglas, Leighton Pullan, Percy Dearmer and others. It was a time of Anglo-Russian political reconciliation, and the idea of establishing a better understanding between the Anglican and Orthodox Churches was warmly welcomed by the ecclesiastical leaders in both countries. Walter Frere took a keen interest in these efforts, and gladly accepted an invitation to deliver a course of addresses in Russia on the life of the Anglican Church. He made most careful preparations for this journey, and he learned enough Russian to be able to read and to understand that language. While in Russia he spent several weeks in a convent near Riga, living with the family of a deacon and thus becoming familiar with the mentality of ordinary members of the Russian Church.

The fruit of his studies was the book entitled *Links in the Chain of Russian Church History* (London: Faith Press), which he published in 1918. It reveals a remarkable grasp of the main trends in the life and thought of Orthodox Christians. His lectures addressed to the St. Petersburg audience were also published in English and in Russian,[2] and they help their readers to understand the main reasons for his interest in reunion with the East.

These earliest associations with the Russian Orthodoxy were brought to an abrupt end by the outbreak of the Communist Revolution in 1917 which swept away Imperial Russia and most of those people who had welcomed Walter Frere to their Russian homes, and for some of whom he felt a profound affection. (He became particularly friendly with

[1] See Fourth Annual Report of the Anglican and Eastern Orthodox Churches Union, 1912, p. 36.

[2] *English Church Ways* (described to Russian friends in four lectures delivered in St. Petersburg in March 1914 by W. H. Frere). (London: John Murray, 1914); and *The Life of the Anglican Church* (in Russian). (Y.M.C.A. Press: Paris, 1930.)

Pavel Mansurov, the author of a remarkable little book called *The Russian Church in* 1915, published by the Anglican and Foreign Church Society in 1917.) It seemed that the cause to which he gave so much of his heart and mind had no chance of any further development.

But unexpectedly Frere was called to participate once more in the same work, and even to play a more leading role in the relations between the Anglican and Eastern Orthodox Communions. This new phase was inaugurated in 1928 when he was elected the first Anglican President of the Fellowship of St. Alban and St. Sergius.

This Fellowship came into being as an expression of a spontaneous desire on the part of the members of a small conference which was held in the St. Alban's Diocesan Retreat House from 28th Dec. 1927 to 2nd Jan. 1928.[1] That conference was the second one organized by the Student Movements of Great Britain and the Russian Student Movement in Exile. (The first one was also held in St. Albans, in Jan. 1927.) Its purpose was to give an opportunity for the younger representatives of the Orthodox, Anglican, and Free Church traditions to compare their experience and outlook.

Though the majority of its members were students, it included several prominent theologians, such as Bishop Gore and Bishop Frere on the Anglican side, and Rev. Prof. S. Bulgakov, Prof. N. Arseniev and Prof. S. Bezobrazov on the Russian.

This informal conference was an experiment in Reunion work which discovered a new road towards that inspiring and yet difficult goal. The conference had its centre neither in the animated debates nor in the learned addresses, but in the worship in the Chapel where, on alternate days, the Anglican and the Eastern Orthodox Eucharist was celebrated. Such a participation in the prayer-life of another tradition was a revolutionary experience for both Anglicans

[1] See printed Report of the Conference published by the Student Christian Movement of Gt. Britain and Ireland, 1928.

WALTER HOWARD FRERE

and Orthodox. Many misunderstandings and even deep-rooted prejudices were removed in this way, and a genuine sense of unity was achieved which led to the formation of the Fellowship. Bishop Frere impressed every member of the conference so much that he was unanimously invited to become the President of the newly-formed Society. He willingly consented, and this started the second period of his relations with the Russian Church, lasting until his death in 1938, and reaching its culminating point in 1936 when, during his visit to Paris, Bishop Frere sang in the Russian Cathedral an Anglican Litany for the Russian Congregation.

Bishop Frere was a man of the West. His family tradition, his interests, his upbringing, his mentality, his very gifts were all rooted in the Western tradition, and to an Eastern Christian he seemed to be the very incarnation of the spirit of Western Christianity. And yet his love for Russian Orthodoxy was profound and genuine, and his concern for the reunion of the West and the East played an important part in his life. Walter Frere's appreciation of Eastern Christianity was not the result of discontent with his own tradition, nor was it the emotional attraction towards the East which is sometimes noticeable among members of the Western Churches—the Anglican in particular.

In his lectures delivered in St. Petersburg he gave a most illuminating account of the inner reasons which promoted his lively concern for reunion with the East. He revealed in them that, while aware of the difficulties confronting the work of Unity, he was conscious of the contribution which the Christian East could make to the Anglican Church, and yet at the same time convinced that his own Communion possessed values needed by other Churches. He was proud of the great Western tradition which he represented in such an accomplished manner.

Here are some extracts from these lectures of his:

'Nothing is more necessary than that East and West should again understand one another, and few things are more difficult. The difficulty is specially great for us British people. We are at the extreme edge of the West in temperament as well as in geography.'[1]

'Our way is different from that to which you are accustomed, yet it is the way in which God has led us. . . . Our ideal has had a great tradition, and we Anglicans believe that it still has a future before it, and especially a part to play in the future reunion of Christendom, for which we all pray.'[2]

'One of the reasons why now, and in earlier days, we have tried to know more of the Eastern Church, is because we wish to be free of one-sidedness and to enter into a wider and fuller appreciation of that common Catholic and Orthodox Faith which we all alike hold, though we look at it from different angles according to our different history and capacity.'[3]

Walter Frere was a Catholic in the deepest and truest sense of the word, and his longing for the restoration of unity between the East and the West sprang from his belief that this alone could rescue Christians from that one-sided sectarian outlook which is both the root and the main consequence of Church divisions.

He discerned in the history of Western Christendom two dangerous tendencies which distorted its development and stopped its intercourse with the Christian East. These were too great a reliance upon Aristotle in theology and an equally strong tendency towards legalism in dogmatic thought and ecclesiastical organization. Both these defects were (according to his mind) provoked by the same cause—the exaggerated self-confidence of the man of the West in his own intellectual ability and power. This pride brought about first the split between Rome and the East, and later, provoked the revolt of the Reformation.

Bishop Frere represented the Anglican position as a legitimate protest against the one-sidedness of Western medieval tradition, and he considered the reunion with the

[1] *English Church Ways*, p. 3.
[2] Ibid., p. 8.
[3] Ibid, p. 11.

Orthodox Church as a part of a general move towards the restoration of the fullness of Catholic life.

He was particularly interested in those Christians whose history and mentality were shaped under different historical conditions, and who were therefore free from specifically Western limitations. The Russian Church intrigued him, sometimes puzzled him, and always stimulated him; for she was the least Western of all the main living branches of the Catholic Church. In his article in the *Church Times* (19th June 1914) which described his impressions of the Russian Church, he wrote, 'To a Western mind the lack of dogmatic sense of sequence and climax in the Orthodox Liturgy is very puzzling. We are inclined to ask, "Why have so much magnificence early in the Service, e.g. at the Offertory, or so much evidence of devotion there and so little after the Consecration? Why choose the place between consecration and communion as the time at which to preach your sermon?" And so on. Possibly such questions surprise the Russian quite as much as the things questioned surprise the Englishman. Probably he merely replies, "Why not? the Liturgy is all one piece—a little bit of time, linked to Eternity".'

In the second part of the same article he developed further the same thoughts: 'Again, we try to grasp the conception which the Orthodox Church has of itself and of its own authority. Our instinct is to turn to the clergy, for clericalism is one of those medieval legacies of the Western schism which we have never shed: and in consequence we confuse Church authority with clerical authority. But we find the Russian clergy as mainly ministers of worship and sacrament. They are not necessarily the teachers; the professor of dogmatic theology is commonly a layman.'

In these passages Bishop Frere reveals himself as a man deeply rooted in his own tradition and yet capable of understanding the point of view arising from an entirely different background. An outlook puzzling at first, and yet belonging to the Catholic treasure of the Universal Church, and therefore a source of joy and enrichment for all its true members.

There were two special features of Russian Christianity which impressed him greatly: its timelessness and the vivid sense of the Communion of Saints which he observed among the ordinary Russian Christians. He also greatly loved Russian Church Music, which he described as 'lifting the congregation off from its pedestrian level and setting it soaring'.

Bishop Frere was always reticent. His articles commenting on his visit to Russia contain no high-sounding words about the importance of the work for Reunion, yet the significance which he attributed to it can be judged by his study of Russian Church History. He made it with the same thoroughness and scholarly perfection as he showed in all his other writings. His little book, *Some Links in the Chain of Russian History*, about which he once remarked that hardly anyone ever read it, is a piece of serious research work. Bishop Frere read the early Russian Chronicles in the original, and made himself familiar with all the best Russian works on the history of their Church. It was not an easy undertaking, but he mastered it with complete success. *Some Links* is not only a monument of his scholarship but also of his deep grasp of Russian mentality, so strikingly different in many respects from his own tradition and upbringing.

The gift so to understand the Russians as to be trusted and loved by them he displayed once more when he became the President of the Fellowship of St. Alban and St. Sergius. At first the Fellowship was a very small and informal body, mostly limited, on the Russian side, to the Professors and Students of the Theological College in Paris, and, on the Anglican, to the younger clergy. Bishop Frere, absorbed in the exacting duties of his episcopal office had neither time nor many opportunities for shewing definite leadership in this work. Nevertheless he seldom failed to appear at the Annual Conferences of the Fellowship, and to give his advice and assistance on those occasions when such were required from him. His vivid interest in the work, even in those early stages of its development, was clearly shewn by the time and close attention he gave to the production of

'A Brief Form of Corporate Prayer from Eastern Sources, for use on various occasions.'[1] A. F. Dobbie Bateman, who worked with the Bishop on the text and the music of this Office, wrote in 1938:[2] 'Bishop Frere worked over every iota of the text, fitted the chants, criticized the set-up. St. Mary's Press had to match his patience with detail.' The Bishop himself in the preface to this little Prayer Book formulated in the following way his appreciation of these corporate efforts of the several members of the Fellowship:

'This is not an anthology of Eastern Prayers, though it is desirable that we Anglicans should be more familiar than we are with the great Treasure Houses of Orthodox worship. It is a Service which has grown up from the practical need of a form of short corporate prayer in which all the Fellowship of St. Alban and St. Sergius could share. The prayers seem in form to be Eastern, the music to be Western, while the language is in English. But in practice, this medley has been found to have a devotional value of its own. It is now therefore printed and issued not only for the use of the Fellowship, but of any others also who may value it, especially as a token of growing Unity.

'*St. Andrew's Day*, 1934.

This short preface is very characteristic of its author. It expresses well his catholicity of outlook, his keen concern for unity, and his equally strong conviction that worship is the best channel leading towards that goal.

The publication of the Corporate Prayer was the beginning of his much more active participation in the work of the Fellowship. It coincided with the animated discussion among its members as to the possibility of intercommunion between Anglican and Orthodox, opened by Father Sergius Bulgakov

[1] Published in 1934 at St. Mary's Press, Wantage, obtainable from 52 Ladbroke Grove, W.11, price 1s. 6d.
[2] *Sobornost*, journal of the Fellowship, N 14, June 1938, p. 4.

at the Fellowship Conference in June 1933 at High Leigh.

Fr. Bulgakov's proposal deeply stirred everybody. It was prophetic and provocative at the same time, as were all other ideas emanating from that daring Christian thinker and devout Orthodox Priest.

He proposed that those Orthodox and Anglican members of the Fellowship who find themselves in doctrinal agreement should enter as a group in communion with another, but, in order to make this action an act of solemn reconciliation between the divided parts of the Church, each member of these groups should first receive the imposition of the Bishop's hands bestowing sacramental blessing on behalf of that body with which he was about to enter into communion.[1]

This call for Liturgical action raised a number of doctrinal, liturgical and canonical questions of far-reaching importance, which were keenly debated by the members of the Fellowship. It soon became quite clear that 'the molecular reunion' (such was the name given to this proposal) had ardent supporters and, as well, equally determined opponents. This division in no way coincided with confessional allegiance, and both parties contained members of Orthodox and Anglican Churches. It was also obvious that everyone was particularly keen to secure the support of the President, who seemed to be specially qualified to act as an arbiter in the solution of an issue so perplexing and yet so vital.

Bishop Frere, however, was at first reluctant to commit himself to any pronouncement. He felt that the proposal needed further study and elucidation. He was particularly keen to know more details about the practical application of the scheme. It was to a large extent due to his insistence that, on the recommendation of the senior members, the Second Fellowship Conference of 1934 adopted a resolution which suggested a further study of the whole problem. It contained among other points the following statement: 'How does the proposal affect the Bishop? clergy? laity? Who should be the celebrant? Would it be on very special occasions or in

[1] For further detail see *Sobornost*, N 3. Sept. 1935, p. 12 *sq.*

general?'[1] Behind these questions was Bishop Frere with his lucid mind and love for precision.

The answers he received from the supporters of the scheme did not satisfy him entirely, and he stated this publicly at the Conference of 1935 (25th–27th June), where he was one of the chief speakers. Its main subject was 'The Nature of Catholic Action', and Bishop Frere, speaking after Father Bulgakov, said among other things: 'There is a need for perspective. Some of our divisions are 1500 years old. They will not be healed very quickly.... We must also avoid getting "swelled heads" and exaggerating the importance of our own small and very young Fellowship. ...' With regard to the proposals of Fr. Bulgakov he thought that 'they were still too vague and needed elucidation. They would require considerable expansion before they could be submitted to the authorities. Why not treat the proposals as having had a first reading and now to be gone into by the Fellowship "in Committee" (to use parliamentary language) and discussed clause by clause?'[2] The Conference after very lively debates arrived at the conclusion 'That the time has not yet come for us to promote any scheme of intercommunion'.[3] It made, however, a number of recommendations for the further study of the whole problem. Soon after, the President of the Fellowship resigned his see, and it was as simply Bishop Frere that he came to Paris, where the Fellowship had its Conference from 30th Dec.–3rd Jan. 1936, at the Château de Quincy. Walter Frere surprised many of his friends by his new attitude to the burning question with which the Fellowship had been preoccupied for the last three years. In France, relieved from the responsibility of his diocesan office, free from the party controversies which made special caution necessary in every pronouncement affecting such questions as orders or intercommunion, Bishop Frere suddenly revealed himself more in favour of the original proposal than had appeared so far

[1] See the Journal of the Fellowship, Sept. 1934, N 25, p. 7.
[2] See Report of the Conference, *Sobornost*, N 3, pp. 18–19.
[3] Ibid., p. 20.

to the rest of the members. In his remarkable opening address he said: 'We Anglicans are here in Paris feeling somewhat *depaysés*. Sometimes it is of great value to be free. This is the first time that we are present at a Fellowship Meeting as individuals. We have something big to contribute to the main problem before us, so that perhaps our hopes and plans for intercommunion, if we attack them as individuals, and view them as individuals, will succeed better than if we consider them as a group.'[1]

These were revealing words, for Bishop Frere could speak and act for the first time unhampered by his official position. He confirmed them by an impressive act of public worship when on 1st January 1936 he sang a Litany[2] in the Russian Cathedral in Paris. Vested in cope and mitre, he stood in the traditional place of an Orthodox Bishop, in the middle of a packed Orthodox congregation. This service was the culminating point in the long history of his relations with the Russian Orthodox Church. It is highly significant that the Orthodox congregation at once accepted him, and treated him as one of their own bishops. Few of the Russians gathered in that church had much knowledge about the Anglican Communion; even fewer had any clear idea as to who the man was who chanted strange prayers to even stranger music; but they all felt that that tall old bishop who presided over them with such natural dignity and devotion was one of themselves. As soon as the service was over a crowd of people rushed to ask the Bishop's blessing, and kissed his hand—according to the Orthodox custom. This spontaneous demand for episcopal benediction sealed the years of labour and prayer which Walter Frere dedicated to the cause of Unity.

He met his Orthodox friends once more in the April of the same year (1936), when several professors from the Russian Theological College in Paris were invited to visit the

---

[1] *Sobornost*, N 5, March 1936, p. 2.
[2] Was this the Prayer Book Litany, sung to the exquisite Sarum plainsong setting? One likes to think so: and it is more than probable. [C.S.P.]

Community of the Resurrection at Mirfield, and confer there with some Anglican theologians. It was a profitable meeting. Bishop Frere was in the chair, but his physical strength was obviously declining and he did not pursue the subject he raised in Paris. The words then spoken proved to be more a prophecy for some future action than a plan which he could realize in his own life.

Such were Bishop Frere's contacts with the Orthodox Church, and they give rise to the general question as to why he felt so much at home among the Russian Christians, and why they so easily and lovingly accepted him as their leader, and recognized in him a bishop of the Catholic Church. This question needs an answer, for in many ways Walter Frere represented an outlook and culture so drastically different from the Russian that it might appear to be irreconcilably opposed to the latter. The unexpected affinity between him and the Russian Orthodox throws an illuminating light upon the whole problem of Anglo-Orthodox relations.

Bishop Frere was a Western Christian, and he was also the most typical representative of that distinct Christian tradition which can be described under the term 'Anglicanism'. He was Catholic and Evangelical at the same time, and both his Catholicism and Evangelicalism were of an unmistakably Anglican type. The distinct mark of both is the emphasis on freedom, which is often combined with pragmatism, or, if one looks at it from another angle, is based on a firm trust in the power of the Holy Spirit. This outlook made Frere suspicious of any rigid formulæ, and of too logical, and still more, too legal presentation of Christian truth.

In spite of his clear and precise mind he knew that life is deeper and more mysterious than our knowledge of it, and he himself in the following way formulated that side of the Anglo-Orthodox co-operation which presented to him its special attraction:

'The great task of Orthodox and Catholic Christianity is to discern in every age what part of its activity and power belongs to that portion of itself which is permanent, unchanging and inalienable, and to maintain those inviolable; while at the same time giving free play to all those moving, progressing and developing forces within itself which life, just because it is life, exhibits in a continual state of energetic and purposeful change. The Church must keep that which is fixed fixed, and leave that which is free free.'[1]

It was this spirit of Christian freedom, combined with deep love and reverence for tradition which he possessed in such an extraordinary way, that brought Bishop Frere so close to the life of the Orthodox Church. He and his Russian friends were baptized by the same Spirit, and they recognized each other as members of the same body, though on the human level they belonged to two quite different cultures. It was this unity in the deepest strata of spiritual experience, which existed in spite of divergence in all other spheres of life, that made the encounter between Walter Frere and the Orthodox Christians so stimulating and challenging to both sides.

Bishop Frere was a man of singular integrity. Everything artificial, merely intellectual or emotional could never have any place in his life. His life-long interest in Russian Christianity sprang from the depth of his spiritual being. The Orthodox East and Anglicanism met in his person and recognized each other as members of the same Body of Christ.

There could be no better tribute to this deep sense of oneness which the Orthodox felt for Bishop Frere than the letter written by Father Sergius Bulgakov to Father Geoffrey Curtis, C.R., on 9th April 1938:

My dear Fr. Curtis,

First of all I want to express to you how deeply I was grieved by the death of Bishop Walter Frere, that righteous and saintly man, a true Christian who was humble in heart and wise in mind, a prominent scholar, an outstanding Churchman, and my dear friend.

[1] *English Church Ways*, p. 106.

It was always a joy to meet him, and a consolation to col-
laborate with him. It was a moral support to find in him a
friend and adviser.

He was particularly destined to become the Head of the
Anglo-Orthodox Fellowship. He was called to understand
Anglicanism at its best, in its combination of faithfulness to
the tradition of the Church and spiritual freedom. This loss of
our Chairman and leader, of a father and a friend, will be
irreparable for the Fellowship. His appearance in the midst
of us was always a joy and inspiration. I remember with particular warmth his last visit to Paris and his attendance at the
Anglo-Russian Conference at Quincy after which he offici-
ated at a short Anglican Service in our Cathedral at Rue
Daru, and was present at dinner in St. Sergius House. . . .

In his person piety and sincerity of soul were combined
with childlike serenity, high culture and personal gentleman-
ship of the most attractive kind. I do not feel prepared to
estimate the significance of his death for the life and work of
the Community of the Resurrection, but I ask you to express
to all members of the Community, including their Head, the
highly-esteemed Father Talbot, my deep sympathy in this
heavy loss.

Requiescat in Pace, et Ora Pro Nobis.

Yours affectionately,

S. BULGAKOV.

P.S.—Next Tuesday the Metropolitan Eulogius with his
clergy (myself included) will officiate a solemn Requiem
Service in St. Sergius Church within the walls of our House.[1]

It is hardly possible to add anything to these words, for
they sum up perfectly the place which Bishop Frere won in
the hearts of his Orthodox friends and the love which they
felt for the man who served God and the Church with the
single devotion of a pure and holy life.

[1] The original wording of the letter is retained, its English remaining
uncorrected.

12

BACK TO MIRFIELD

by C. S. Phillips

Lhe sequel of Frere's episcopate was quite different from that of Gore's. It is very doubtful whether Gore ever greatly enjoyed being a bishop, and quite certain that he laid down the burden of diocesan work with the relief and delight of a schoolboy off for the holidays. Frere, on the other hand, despite all trials and disappointments, undoubtedly found much that was congenial in the episcopal office (at least on its pastoral side), and especially when, as the years went on, he felt more and more sure of the confidence and affection of both clergy and laity, with the exception of a small number of *enragés* whom nothing would ever propitiate. When at last he gave up, it was simply because his conscience told him that he was no longer equal to the work. Thus whereas Gore, in exchanging Cuddesdon Palace for what he called his 'hov-*el*' in London, was to enter on a period that was in some ways the happiest and most fruitful of his life, Frere on leaving Truro more or less vanished from view, apart from a momentary and distinctly challenging emergence at the very end when his remarkable book on *The Anaphora* was published early in 1938. Inevitably, it was to Mirfield that he betook himself. He might sometimes have talked of retiring to South Africa, where he could 'be warm', and even (but this, of course, only by way of a castle in the air) of spending his last years in some pleasant old South German city, where he could go to the opera or a concert every night! But, in the end, both duty and sentiment drew him back to the place on the bleak West Riding hillside from which he had never been separated except in a purely spatial sense. As he said, he had 'come home'.

Awaiting him at Mirfield was a small group of very senior members of the Community—all survivors of the old days at Radley and theoretically entitled to certain privileges with regard to diet, etc., suitable to their advanced years. Thus James Nash (back from many years as a bishop in South Africa), Walter Frere, George Longridge, Gerard Sampson and Paul Bull found themselves all together once more. But the privileges of age seemed to make very little appeal to any of them, and perhaps to 'Father Walter' least of all; with the result that their regimen was in practice exactly the same as that of everybody else.

In other ways too, despite his steadily growing infirmities, Frere partook fully in the common life. By way of recreation he had a wireless set which, by a special concession, he was allowed to keep in his room, with a gramophone on which he loved to play his by now large and choice collection of records. Occasionally (at least at first) he went away to preach or to take a retreat: and in Christmas Week 1935 we have already seen him as far afield as France, presiding over a Conference of the Fellowship of St. Alban and St. Sergius. He even managed, only a few months before his death, to get down to Truro for the Jubilee of the Dedication of the Cathedral and to preach in it once again at the Sung Eucharist on Sunday, 7th Nov. In the course of a few days' stay he saw a number of old friends, and was able to spend an evening with his beloved 'Bark Choir', still functioning vigorously (though no longer at Lis Escop) and adhering with an almost religious fidelity to the old arrangements, including the ban on practice and repetition.

By way of holiday he had the two motoring tours in the late summer of 1935 and 1936 already spoken of. In the September of 1937 he spent a week with his old friend Sydney Nicholson at Woodchurch in Kent: but it was clear

IN RETIREMENT, 1936

by that time that he had not much longer to live. He was
glad to go out and visit some churches; but, unless the
church was something very exceptional, he was content to
remain sitting in the car and to accept the report on the
interior brought back by his companions.

So, to the accompaniment of great physical weakness and
pain, his iron will dragged him somehow through the winter
of 1937–8, including the long journey to Cornwall. To the
end he fought against any mitigation of the discipline that
he had chosen. A day or two before he died Fr. Horner put
his head round the door of his room to ask which of two
alternative ways of increasing his comfort he would prefer.
'I think', came the crisp, humorous voice from the bed, 'I
would prefer to do what I'm told.'

Of Frere's last years at Mirfield Fr. Talbot writes as
follows:

'Nothing was more notable in Frere than the silence that
covered the disappointments of his life and the mortifications
that he either accepted or imposed upon himself. In the pur-
suit of some of the main objectives he set before himself he
encountered what must have been acute disappointment.
And one may guess at but not measure the severity of the
mortification with which he disciplined himself. Yet all this
was borne and carried through with so blithe an air that it
might seem as though there were no self-denial in it—and
that it was just natural to him to do so easily what most men
could hardly do at all: or, if they did, they would be sure to
make some little parade of their effort or indulge some small
consoling touch of self-pity. Such parade and such indul-
gence Frere never allowed himself. It was under the cover of
this silence and seeming insouciance that he met the growing
weakness and failing powers of the last years of his life. He
was very frail and worn. The natural force used without stint
or waste throughout the years was being spent to its last
ounce until there was no more to spend. Physical discom-
forts and distresses were upon him; food was distasteful; and
even his iron control could not altogether conceal the fact of

ɔled body and irritable nerves. Some of the bright-
ɔs dimmed; some of the patience exhausted. But to the
ɔ maintained the order and industry of his life. Regu-
he took his place in choir, though often it was only too
.dent how great a tax it levied on his strength. Only in the
.st two months could he be persuaded, most unwilling, to
give up climbing up and down the steep steps to the crypt,
where at that time the Community services had perforce to
be held. When at last this became impossible, he was always
up and ready for the Mass that was said daily in his room
until three days before he died. "I live by that," he said. In
the last year of his life he wrote a book which, whatever dis-
agreement it meets, lacks nothing in lucidity and pungency.
Five days before his death he was delivering a lecture to the
College students; and was busy drawing up a service of
Dedication of the Community church. Occasionally one
caught a glimpse of a darkness upon the spirit that is the last
test of a soul's fidelity. But light-footed he had trod this
world, even while with all diligence he plied the tasks which
God ordained for him. He walked with the untrammelled
independence of one awake to sights and sounds beyond the
world. Gently he passed from it on 2nd April 1938.'

The funeral took place in the Community church at Mirfield on Wednesday, 6th April. A Solemn Requiem was celebrated by the Superior (Fr. Talbot) in the presence of four
bishops—the Bishop of Truro (Dr. Hunkin), who travelled
all the way to Yorkshire for the purpose, the Bishop of
Pontefract (also representing the Bishop of Wakefield, who
was ill), and Bishops Nash and Mounsey of the Community
—together with a large company of clergy. The body was
subsequently cremated. On the same day Solemn Requiems
were also sung in Truro Cathedral and at All Saints',
Margaret Street.

The ashes rest within a plain stone altar-tomb on the
south side of the sanctuary at Mirfield, with horizontal bands
in the upper part of each of its sides bearing the inscription
in gilt letters on a turquoise ground:

THE TOMB AND IKON

BACK TO MIRFIELD

+ WALTER . SUPERIOR . EPISCOPUS +
NAT. 1863. PROF. 1892. OB. 2 APRIL 1938.

On the north side a similar tomb contains the ashes of
Charles Gore. Thus the 'pioneer' and the 'consolidator' keep
guard on either side of the high altar of their Community
church.

After the tomb was completed a triptych painted in delicate, clear colours in the ikon manner was set up on the wall
above the altar facing its eastern foot, representing the
Ascended Christ in the centre panel with small medallions of
St. Alban and St. Sergius on either side, and St. Basil and
St. Seraphim on the wings. It was painted on the spot by a
Russian nun—a silent figure in sweeping black robes who
for a period of some months might be seen passing in and
out of the Community church, herself and her work a symbol of the newly-forged links between the Church of England
and the ancient Christianity of the East, both so dear to
Frere's heart.

In Truro Cathedral the Bishop is commemorated by a
noble brass on the floor of the south choir aisle, designed by
the Vicar of St. Peter's, Newlyn, whom he had himself
ordained. He is represented in mitre and eucharistic vestments: his right hand is raised in benediction, while his left
hand holds his staff, the crook of which bears the Agnus Dei,
the badge of the Community of the Resurrection. Round
the four sides runs the inscription:

IN PIAM MEMORIAM WALTER HOWARD FRERE. D.D.
COMMUNITATIS RESURRECTIONIS OLIM SUPERIORIS.
EPISCOPI TRURONENSIS MCMXXIII—MCMXXXV.
ECCE SACERDOS MAGNUS.[1]

---

[1] The last three words (in English, 'Behold, a great Priest') are from the
Office for the Common of a Bishop. The brass is the first and smaller part of
the whole memorial. It is intended to complete this by the erection of the
'Bishop Frere Muniment Room' on the east side of the north transept; but
here the war has compelled postponement.

LIST OF WRITINGS

Abbreviations: AC = Alcuin Club (–C = Collections, –P = Pamphlets, –$PBRP$ = Prayer Book Revision Pamphlets, –T = Tracts). c = Reprinted in whole or in part in 'W.H.F.: a collection of his papers' (*see below p.* 6). CHS = Church Historical Society. CQR = Church Quarterly Review. C & YS = Canterbury and York Society. HBS = Henry Bradshaw Society. JTS = Journal of Theological Studies. P & MMS = Plain song and Mediaeval Music Society. *Rev.* = Review. TDG = Truro Diocesan Gazette.

Where no place of publication is stated after a *book*, 'London' is to be understood.

General and Local History

1890   Memorials of Stepney parish . . . the Vestry Minutes, from 1579 to 1662 . . . ed. by G. W. Hill and W.H.F. (Pr. for subscribers.)
Guildford.

„   A sketch of the parochial history of Barley, Herts. . . . by A. and W.H.F. *Stepney Green.*

1892   Two centuries of Stepney history, 1480–1680. Three lectures. . . .

1895   c   The place of the Papacy in the organization of Christian unity. (Notes of a speech. . . .)

1896   What is the position of the Roman Catholic body in England? (*CHS Publ.* 5.)

„   The Marian reaction in its relation to the English clergy. A study of the episcopal Registers. (*CHS Publ.* 18.)

LIST OF WRITINGS

1898   Lancelot Andrewes as a representative of Angli-
        can principles: a lecture. . . . (*CHS Publ.*
        44.)

1903   The relation of Church and Parliament in regard
        to ecclesiastical discipline.   *Oxford.*

1904   The English Church in the reigns of Elizabeth
        and James I, 1558–1625. (Hist. of the Eng.
        Ch., ed. by W. R. W. Stephens and W. Hunt,
        vol. 5.)

1907   Puritan manifestoes. A study of the origin of the
        Puritan revolt. . . . Ed. by W.H.F. and C. E.
        Douglas. (*CHS Publ.* 72.)

1909   The early history of Canons Regular as illus-
        trated by the foundation of Barnwell Priory.
        (*In* Fasciculus I. W. Clark dicatus, pp. 186–
        216.)   *Cambridge.*

1910 c Lollardy and the Reformation. [*Rev. of* Lollardy
        and the Reformation, by J. Gairdner, *and other
        works.*] (*CQR* lxix 426–39.)

  ,,   Visitation articles and injunctions of the period of
        the Reformation. Ed. by W.H.F. 3 vols. (*ACC*
        14–16.)   *Oxford.*

1912   [*Articles on*] Advertisements—Elizabethan Settle-
        ment—Feckenham (J. de)—Gilpin (B.)—Grin-
        dal (E.)—Harpsfield (N.)—Heath (N.)—
        Hymns—Injunctions—Kitchin (A.)—Marian
        Reaction—Ornaments Rubric—Parker (M.)
        —Roman Catholics—Whitgift (J.). (*In* A
        Dictionary of English Church history, ed. by
        S. L. Ollard . . . G. Crosse.)

1913 c Some vicissitudes of English parochial history.
        (*CQR* lxxvi 308–32.)

1914   Registrum Iohannis Whyte Episcopi Wintonen-
        sis, MDLVI–MDLIX. With a prefatory note by
        W.H.F. (*C & YS* 16.)   *Oxford.*

1916   East and West. (*In* Our place in Christendom:
        lectures. . . . Pp. 18–44.)

205

1918 Some links in the chain of Russian Church history.

1925 The modern history of the Church of England. (Little Books on Religion, 38.)

„ Bennett (F.S.M.): The nature of a cathedral. (With introd. by W.H.F.) *Chester*.

1928–35 Registrum Matthei Parker, diocesis Cantuariensis, A.D. 1559–75 . . . ed. with an introd. by W.H.F. 3 vols. (*C & YS* 35, 36, 39.) *Oxford*.

1935 Recollections of Malines.

1937 The Russian Church. (Repr. from 'The Church Assembly News' in 'The Orthodox Church: [by] J. A. Douglas [*and others*]', pp. 23–7.)

Liturgical Publications

1896 The Order of Compline throughout the year, with the musical notation from the Salisbury Antiphonal adapted by G. H. Palmer and W.H.F. *Wantage*.

„ The Wells Office Book. Prime and Hours with other Services for the use of Wells Theological College. [Compiled by W.H.F.] —— (Revised 1914, 1929.)

1898–
1901 The Use of Sarum: i, The Sarum Customs as set forth in the Consuetudinary and Customary. (ii, The Ordinal and Tonal.) The original texts ed. from the MSS with an introd. and index by W.H.F. 2 vols. *Cambridge*.

1899 The Order of Compline from the Sarum Breviary, ed. by W.H.F. and G. H. Palmer.
               Wantage.

„ Exposition de la Messe from La Legende Dorée of Jean de Vignay. With illuminations . . . from Fitzwilliam Mus. MS 22. Ed. by W.H.F. (*ACC* 2.) *Oxford*.

LIST OF WRITINGS

1899   Notes on the early history of the use of incense. (—The post-Reformation uses of incense.) (*In* Westall (H.): The case for incense, pp. 43–85, 137–40, 157–70.)

1900   c   Edwardine vernacular Services before the First Prayer Book. (*JTS* i 229–46.)

1901   Pontifical Services illustrated from miniatures of the fifteenth and sixteenth centuries. With descriptive notes and a liturgical introd. by W.H.F. (*ACC* 3 and 4.)   *Oxford.*

 ,,   c   The newly-found York Gradual. (*JTS* ii 578–86.)

 ,,   A new history of the Book of Common Prayer . . . on the basis of the former work by F. Procter, revised and rewritten by W.H.F. —— (Repr. with corrections, 1902.)

1903   The connexion between English and Norman Rites. (*JTS* iv 206–14.)

 ,,   The English Liturgy: being the Office for Holy Communion . . . with additional Collects, Epistles, and Gospels for the lesser holy-days and for special occasions. . . . Ed. by P. Dearmer, with the assistance of W.H.F. and S. M. Taylor.

1903–4   Rock (D.): The Church of our fathers. . . . A new ed. by G. W. Hart and W.H.F. 4 vols.

1904–15   The Hereford Breviary, ed. . . . by W.H.F. and L. E. G. Brown. 3 vols. (*HBS* 26, 40, 46.)

1906   The principles of religious ceremonial. (Oxford Libr. of Practical Theology.)

1911   Some principles of liturgical reform: a contribution towards the revision of the Book of Common Prayer.

 ,,   c   The Use of Exeter. [*Rev. of* Ordinale Exon, ed. by J. N. Dalton.] (*CQR* lxxiii 137–57.)

1912   The reconstruction of worship. [*Rev. of* The Chronicle of Convocation . . . of Canterbury,— of York, *and other works.*] (*CQR* lxxv 139–60.)

1913   The liturgical Gospels. (*AC PBRP* 2.)

1914   English Church ways described to Russian friends in four lectures . . . at St. Petersburg.

1915   Early Ordination Services. (*JTS* xvi 323–71.)

1916 c The English Rite. [*Rev. of* The English Rite. . . . By F. E. Brightman, *and of* Cranmer's liturgical projects, ed. . . . by J. W. Legg.] (*CQR* lxxxii 283–301.)

1917   The Carolingian Gregorianum; its sections and their numbering. (*JTS* xviii 47–55.)

,,   Russian observations upon the American Prayer Book; transl. by W. J. Barnes and ed. with notes by W.H.F. (*ACT* 12.)

1918   Early forms of Ordination. (*In* Essays on the early history of the Church and the ministry, ed. by H. B. Swete, pp. 263–312.)

1920 c The new South African Liturgy. (*CQR* xc 367–74.)

1921   A relic of St. Willibrord. [*Rev. of* The Calendar of St. Willibrord. . . . Ed. by H. A. Wilson.] (*CQR* xci 356–62.)

,,   The Leofric Collectar. . . . Vol. 2. Ed. and completed . . . by W.H.F. (*HBS* 56.)

1922   The primitive Consecration Prayer; a lecture. . . . (*AC PBRP* 8.)

1925   A liturgical Psalter, arranged for use in the services of the Church by W.H.F.

1926 c The Christian altar. [*Rev. of* J. Braun, Der christliche Altar, *and other works*.] (*CQR* cii 1–19.)

1927 c York Service Books. (York Minster Histor. Tracts 19.)

1930–35 Studies in Early Roman Liturgy. 3 vols. (*ACC* 28, 30, 32.)   *Oxford.*
        i. The Kalendar. 1930.
        ii. The Roman Gospel-Lectionary. 1934.
        iii. The Roman Epistle-Lectionary. 1935.

LIST OF WRITINGS

1935   Collects, Epistles, and Gospels for the Lesser
        Feasts according to the Calendar set out in
        1928, arranged by W.H.F.   *Truro.*
1936 c Early Franciscan influence on religious Ser-
        vices. (Seton Memorial Lecture, 1936.)
1938   Black Letter Saints' days: a companion to 'Col-
        lects, Epistles [*etc.*] . . . in 1928'.
  „   c The Anaphora, or Great Eucharistic Prayer;
        an eirenical study in liturgical history.

Devotional Writings

1896   The stations of the Passion of our Lord and
        Saviour Jesus Christ. Arranged by W.H.F.
                                             Oxford.
1898   Sursum corda: a handbook of intercession and
        thanksgiving arranged by W.H.F. and A. L.
        Illingworth.   *Oxford.*
1905–7 Mirfield Manuals: *Leeds.*
        43 Prayer Book history.—44 The Bible.—
        50 The Little Book of the Contemplation of
        Christ, 1577. St. Augustine's Manual; ed. by
        W.H.F.—51 God's call and man's response.—
        52 Holy Week: the story of the Passion.—
        53 Sutton's Godly Meditations; ed. by W.H.F.
1926   Meditation: a plain guide . . . by W.H.F. and
        G. Longridge. (Little Books on Religion, 42.)
1936   Evelyn (J.): A devotionarie book of J. Evelyn
        . . . now first published, with an introd. by
        W.H.F. (Ed. of 250 copies.)

Diocesan Papers
(published in the 'Truro Diocesan Gazette')

1924   Address to first Diocesan Conference. (July)
        Advent to Christmas. (Dec.)

o   209

1925   The modern history of the Church of England, explained in a letter to a French friend. (Jan.—March)

Some great books of religion. (Feb.—Dec.)

First Pastoral letter. (March)

1926   On singing *Veni, Creator*. (Jan.)

c The Gloria in excelsis. (March)

c The end of the celebration of Holy Communion. (April)

c The Oblations. (May)

The reform of Church Courts. (Aug.)

1927 c Reservation in Elizabethan days. (April)

Article on Episcopal Visitations. (April & May)

The return to theology. (July)

c The new Consecration Prayer. (Nov.)

1928   The Archbishop's message.—Enrolment.—Useful forms. (Jan.)

Christian reunion.—Woodard schools. (March)

The new Prayer Book. (April)

The Prayer Book. (May)

Who should decide? (June)

c The authority for Reservation. (Aug.)

1929   Cornish Saints. (March)

The prebendal church of St. Endellion. (May)

The latest Cornish hagiology. (Nov.)

1930   Conditional Ordination. (Feb.)

Parochial and ecclesiastical boundaries. (April)

The Scottish Prayer Book. (Aug.)

Rules for Transcription of Registers. (Dec.)

1931 c Funerals. (April)

c Collects good and bad. (May)

c Climax and anti-climax. (June)

Intercession for a troubled world. (July)

Christian marriage. (Aug.)

1932   Prevention is better than cure. [Article on purity.] (Jan.)

Music and worship. (March)

Peace in our time. (Aug.)
The ministry of women. (Nov.)
Religious plays. (Dec.)

1933 Lay or cleric. (Jan.)
The moral requisites for trade revival. (Feb.)
Employment. (March)
Mistrust and fear. (April)
Union of benefices. (May)
A eucharistic hymn, *Adoro te devote*. (Aug.)
Kalendar of Celtic Saints. (Sept.)
Parochial boundaries. (Oct.)
Helps and hindrances in public worship.—Charles
Henderson, an appreciation. (Nov.)

1934 c The pace of Responses. (Jan.)
Recollections of Malines. (March, etc. *Subsequently published in book form.*)
[He wrote in addition notes on diocesan business,
on pastoral problems, on current affairs, reviews
of books, and short articles on a great variety
of topics.]

Music

1885 Shelley (P. B.): Love's philosophy. Solo and
pianoforte setting by W.H.F. (*In* Mag. of
Music. 'The Harp Supplement.' Sept. 1885.)

[188–] Two country songs of Dorsetshire: poetry by W.
Barnes, music by Walter Frere.

1888 Eighteen well-known hymn-tunes, as set in
Ravenscroft's Psalter (1621) reprinted . . .
with reference to their use in Hymns A. and M.
and Church Hymns. Ed. by W.H.F.

1890 The Order of the Holy Communion set to music
in unison for men's voices. [1890.]

[189–?] Vitorelli (Jacopo): Three Italian songs. Solo and
parts, set by W.H.F. ('Ecco, ritorna il mese.'—
'O platano felice.'—'Guarda che bianca luna.')
[*No date.*]

1894   The Winchester Troper from MSS of the tenth and eleventh centuries, with other documents illustrating the history of Tropes in England and France. Ed. by W.H.F. (*HBS* 8.)

1894   Graduale Sarisburiense: a . . . facsimile of a MS of the thirteenth cent. (Brit. Mus. MS Add 12194), with a dissertation and historical index illustrating its historical development from the Gregorian Antiphonale Missarum, by W.H.F. (*P & MMS.*)

1895   [*Lectures on*] Tonality—Hymnody—Music of the Holy Eucharist—Accompaniment. (*In* The Elements of Plainsong. Compiled from lectures delivered before . . . the Plainsong and Mediæval Music Soc. Ed. by H. B. Briggs.) (*P & MMS.*)

1896   Hymn-melodies for the whole year from the Sarum Service-books and other ancient English sources, together with Sequences for the principal seasons and festivals. (Ed. by W.H.F.) *P & MMS.*)   *Wantage.*

1898–   Rossetti (Christina): Six songs from the 'The Face
1900   of the Deep' set by W.H.F. ('Song of the Martyrs.'—'Song of the Saints.'—'An appeal'. —'None other'.—'In calm or tempest'.— 'Universal praise.') [*Priv. pr.*]

1901–25 Antiphonale Sarisburiense. A . . . facsimile of a MS of the thirteenth century (Cambridge Univ. Libr. Mm. ii. 9), with a dissertation and analytical index by W.H.F. (26 fasc.) (*P & MMS.*)

1901–32 Bibliotheca musico-liturgica. A descriptive handlist of the musical and Latin-liturgical MSS of the Middle Ages . . . in the libraries of Great Britain and Ireland. 2 vols. (*P & MMS.*)

1902   Helmore (T.): A manual of plainsong for Divine Service. Smaller ed., containing the Canticles and Psalter printed for the Gregorian tones together with the Litany and Responses. A new ed. prepared by H. B. Briggs and W.H.F. under the . . . superintendence of J. Stainer.

1909   Hymns Ancient and Modern; historical ed., with notes on the origin of both hymns and tunes and a general historical introduction (by W.H.F.).

1915   The palaeography of early medieval music. [*Rev. of* Monumenti Vaticani di paleografia musicale latina . . . da E. M. Bannister, *and other works.*] (*CQR* lxxxi 137–56.)

„   Songs [12] with music from 'A Child's garden of verses' by R. L. Stevenson. [*Issued anonymously.*]   *Edinburgh.*

1923   Pars Antiphonarii. A . . . facsimile of a MS . . . in the Chapter Library at Durham, MS B. iii. 11. (Introd. by W.H.F.) (*P & MMS.*)

1927–8   [*Articles on*] Antiphon—Antiphonal—Cantor—Cantoris—Gradual—Gregorian Music—Gregorian Tones—Hymn—Hymns Ancient and Modern—Introit—Modes, Ecclesiastical—Plainsong—Psalmody—Responsorial Psalmody—Sequence—Tractus. (*In* Grove's Dict. of Music, 3rd ed. by H. C. Colles, 5 vols.)

1929   Plainsong. (*In* The Oxford Hist. of Music, Introd. vol., ed. by P. C. Buck, pp. 133–63.)

[*Published posthumously*]

1939   An essay in liturgical construction (*In* Anglican Liturgies; ed. by J. H. Arnold . . . pp. 189–94. [*ACT* 22.])   *Oxford.*

1940   Walter Howard Frere: a collection of his papers on liturgical and historical subjects, ed. by J. H. Arnold and E. G. P. Wyatt, with an introd. by A. S. Duncan-Jones. . . . (*ACC* 35.)   *Oxford.*

INDEX

INDEX

INDEX